UN
COMMON
ACCOUNTABILITY

BRIAN P. MORAN
MICHAEL LENNINGTON

UN COMMON

ACCOUNTABILITY

A RADICAL NEW APPROACH

TO GREATER SUCCESS AND FULFILLMENT

WILEY

Published by John Wiley & Sons, Inc., Hoboken, New Jersey.
Published simultaneously in Canada.

For general information on our other products and services or for technical support, please contact our Customer Care Department within the United States at (800) 762-2974, outside the United States at (317) 572-3993 or fax (317) 572-4002.

Wiley also publishes its books in a variety of electronic formats. Some content that appears in print may not be available in electronic formats. For more information about Wiley products, visit our website at www.wiley.com.

Library of Congress Cataloging-in-Publication Data is Available:

ISBN: 9781119764922 (cloth)
ISBN: 9781119764939 (ePub)
ISBN: 9781119764946 (ePDF)

Cover Design: Wiley
Cover Image: © enjoynz/Getty Images

SKY10030295_110521

I would like to dedicate this book to my incredible wife, Judy, and my girls, Gabrielle and Emma. In a life of many blessings, my family is my biggest blessing.

Also, thanks to the many clients who have embraced our concepts and trusted our advice.

— Brian P. Moran

This book is dedicated first and foremost to my wife, Kristin, who made it possible for me to write the thing, and even better, tolerated me while I did so. I also want to thank my children and friends (you know who you are), who challenged and supported me throughout the process of getting to the finish line. Finally, a special acknowledgment to Mike and Mike, who both always understood when I couldn't show up for other things, and to Trevor, who wrote The 12 Week Year for Writers and coached me through the rough bits.

— Michael Lennington

CONTENTS

1

ACCOUNTABILITY AS OWNERSHIP

What if there was one basic human trait that was the foundation of virtually everything that we achieve in life? One characteristic that creates our results, fosters our learning and growth, keeps us sharp and adaptable, builds healthy relationships, improves our mental and physical health, and positively influences nearly everyone that we associate with?

And what if this one thing, this ground-spring of lasting success in life, was also perhaps the most widely misunderstood concept in our culture today? What if the way that most of us think about and apply this fundamental success concept causes many to live a life of mediocrity, disappointment, and frustration rather than the life we are truly capable of? What if the way that most of us engage this concept actually creates the exact opposite of what we desire in life?

If you're like me, you're an avid reader. I learned early on that "leaders are readers," and one particular area of interest for me has always been the strategies, habits, and behaviors of successful people. While I've lost count of all the books that I've read in this genre, some classics like *The 7 Habits of Highly Effective People* by Stephen Covey, as well as more recent works such as *Atomic Habits* by James Clear, stand out to me. In the end, many of these books have positively impacted my success in business, and in life.

Most of the books I've read on this topic identify a set of foundational characteristics and habits that contribute to high achievement. Interestingly, though, many of these works contain different success attributes! While this seemed confusing to me at first, I'm now fine with the variation. The diversity of ideas tells me that there is more than one formula for success in life. That, in and of itself, is encouraging. Over my career, I've applied much of what I learned from these books, and I have benefited greatly.

However, as I have applied the concepts from these books, and developed a few of my own, there is one characteristic that I've found has had by far the greatest impact on my success and my happiness. This one characteristic is common in almost all of the successful people that I've met or studied. It is the one characteristic that is the bedrock of success and achievement. In fact, without it, none of the ideas in all of the books that I've read on self-improvement can deliver on their potential. Yet, this characteristic is also the most frequently misunderstood concept in business and in society today. And this misunderstanding creates the very opposite of what we intend.

I am talking about *personal accountability,* and flipping the way we understand and apply this principle is the mission of this book.

Our experience, working with over one hundred Fortune 1000 companies and tens of thousands of individuals, is that there is a fundamental misperception of what accountability truly is.

Intuitively, most sense that accountability is a good thing, something that leads to better performance and increased results, yet we most often experience accountability as something that is far less than empowering – and in fact is often disempowering. Too often, accountability is synonymous with consequences – in particular, negative consequences. Virtually everywhere you hear accountability mentioned in society, it is typically affiliated with bad behavior, poor performance, and negative consequences. It is a wonder that anyone would want anything to do with it.

Let me give you an example. Let's say a professional athlete does something egregious. What typically happens is that someone in authority – usually the coach or the commissioner – calls a press conference or releases a statement where they assert that they intend to "hold this person accountable" for the offensive actions. Then they fine, suspend, or fire the athlete. In other words, they create some form of negative consequence.

And this approach to accountability is not just reserved for the famous. We all have experienced something like this at various times in our lives. Most often, when accountability is mentioned or practiced it is really just the application of negative consequences.

The costs of this misunderstanding are significant. If we experience accountability as negative consequences and punishment, then it only makes sense that, on an individual level, we would be smart to avoid it. Yet when we shun accountability, there are significant downsides; we often repeat mistakes, miss opportunities, fail to learn and adapt, and generally underperform relative to our potential. At the organizational level, when leaders use negative consequences to shape behavior, they create unintended collateral damage, and ultimately limit individual and group performance. Leaders with this misguided view of accountability create a culture of unmet milestones, missed opportunities, and poor results. The prices of this mindset include lost productivity, lower quality, customer dissatisfaction, low morale, high turnover, lower sales, and diminished profits.

Few words in the English language carry the emotional impact that *accountability* does. Simply mentioning the word can create powerful physiological and emotional responses in the hearer. Accountability has undeniable power to create results, and yet for many people, when it's promoted by someone with authority, the word often elicits anxiety and engenders avoidance behaviors. There is a reason for this *accountability anxiety*, and it starts with the widely promulgated meaning of accountability.

The early 2020 version of Merriam-Webster's online dictionary defines accountability as (emphasis and underlines are mine):

ACCOUNTABLE

1. Subject to giving an account: ANSWERABLE... held her accountable for the damage
2. Capable of being explained: EXPLAINABLE... leaving aside variations accountable as printer errors... – Peter Shaw

Examples of *accountable* in a sentence:

If anything goes wrong, I will hold you personally accountable!

The owner was held accountable for his dog's biting of the child.

Did you notice the hidden assumption evident in each example and definition?

Each one was negative: *damage, errors, goes wrong, dog's biting!* Further, three of the four examples *included the application of negative consequences* to a performer from some unnamed external power or authority. In those examples, one person with authority blames and punishes another person who lacks authority. The authority is active, the person being punished is passive. Accountability as defined above is profoundly asymmetrical.

There were no mentions of the benefits of accountability. No description of personal growth. Nothing about accountability's life-changing power. If you believe the dictionary definitions, you would think that people wanting to take more accountability must first become masochistic. Success, according to *Webster's*, requires punishment!

This traditional view of accountability as punishment creates a power dynamic where authorities seek to assign blame and performers seek to shift it. Accountability in this traditional view is something to be avoided when possible. Further, a person with authority places blame based on the implicit assumption that the performer *intended* to make a mistake or to fall short. What a mess! It's no wonder so many people avoid this view of accountability.

Creating consequences for people when they don't do what you want them to do is not accountability, it's consequence management. Yes, consequences shape behavior but you will never get discretionary effort with negative consequences. You simply get just enough to stop the consequences, *and* it comes with collateral damage, from passive resistance to outright sabotage. Ultimately, we choose our consequences in life by the choices we make every day.

There is another definition of accountability, one that isn't in the dictionary. It is a definition that many people naturally understand and gravitate toward. In this intuitive understanding, personal accountability isn't about negative consequences for poor performance, it's about taking personal ownership of one's state in life. This view of accountability is the foundation of this book.

We either walk our own personal path toward greater accountability, or we don't. No one else can hold us accountable, only we can hold ourselves accountable. In fact, looking for someone else to hold you accountable may be the most unaccountable thing that you can do.

True accountability is based on the realization that we all have free-will choice. By the way, if you think that free will is an illusion and that it does not exist, you are free to hold that belief! For the rest of us who think that we actually do have choices in life, this realization is earth-shattering. If we believe that we "have to" do things, those things naturally become a burden. When we "have to" do something, we feel trapped, coerced into doing things that others want us to do. Life lived with a have-to mindset can begin to feel like a prison.

As soon as we realize that everything is a choice, the prison walls disappear. When we *choose to do something* rather than *have to,* we have a greater sense of personal control and freedom. Obviously, consequences come with every choice. When you take an action (or avoid taking one), you are also choosing the consequences of that action. It's not that consequences are not a part of accountability, it's just that if you are accountable, you see them differently. You realize that you choose your consequences in life.

Your Choices Determine Your Life

"Man is condemned to be free; because once thrown into the world, he is responsible for everything he does. It is up to you to give [life] a meaning." "Freedom is what we do with what is done to us."
— Jean-Paul Sartre

A few years ago, we asked our 12 Week Year community to share with us their personal experiences with our execution system, and while many of the stories were moving, one especially stood out for us. It was the story of how Barbara Shorerock, a retired real estate agent from Alberta, Canada, decided to take ownership of the toughest challenge in her life. What follows is her story in her own words.

At the beginning of 2017, a friend told me about *The 12 Week Year,* and I borrowed the book from the library, and read it. After 22 years of running a real estate business, and 10 years of running my own company before that, *The 12 Week Year* made sense to me. I was used to structure in my life, and planning, and achieving.

But now I was retired. I was looking ahead at the next five years without a need to make sales or to accomplish things financially. That part of my life was set. I couldn't change it now. Now the question before me was, how was I going to operate going forward?

(continued)

(*continued*)

I read *The 12 Week Year* with that in mind. With aspirations for personal things – fitness and health, family, friends, and community – I thought, "I can make that happen." My first 12 weeks were going to be really exciting!

That feeling changed quickly. By the end of February, I learned that I had cancer. By the end of March, at the end of the first 12 weeks, I knew that it was metastatic breast cancer, having already spread to lung and liver, and it was serious.

After the initial shock wore off, I realized that I still had choice about how I would fight my battle and live out the rest of my life, not knowing if that would be a few months, or if I'm fortunate, a number of years.

My new life was all about chemotherapy. Every week, it was up to the chemo clinic, get my chemo injections. Before I even had a chance to implement my "be a better friend" program, I had to call upon my friends and my daughter to drive me around every week. To feed me. To care for me.

After chemo, my choice was to get stronger.

I started up some of the things that I had left behind, such as volunteering for English as a Second Language, volunteering at the theater. I also started walking again, with a goal that by the end of the year I would be able to walk for 60 minutes. My first walk after all the antibiotics was to the end of the block and back.

Other things, like spending time with family, being a better friend, started up again.

(*continued*)

(continued)

It really helped with my life to think about what was in front of me, the choices I still had available to me to do the things that are important to me. The choice to not give into fear of loss, or a lack of time. I can't now, with my new reality, think about a year. But I can think about 12 weeks. I have that choice.

There were two questions that motivated me: "What if?" and "How might I?" Because I was looking forward. I looked at my one-year vision and then put into effect what I can do in the next 12 weeks. That's easy.

It gives my days focus. When I open my day planner and look at a week at a glance and see what's there, I look at where the blank spaces are. There have been times in the last year where there were no blank spaces. Now, I actually have whole days where I can decide what to do with them. I have my goals, and I look at how I fit those in. It gives my days structure, and it gives me focus and purpose.

In spite of the discouraging diagnosis, Barbara never lost sight of the fact that she still had a choice about how to live her life. A little more than a year ago, Barbara's daughter contacted us to let us know that she had passed. When, like Barbara, we look at the choices that are available to us rather than the choices that are not, we retain the freedom to live a life of intentional purpose and fulfillment.

Coming at life from "choose to" rather than "have to" gives you the only control that you have in life. The quality of your choices determines the quality of your life. As Barbara bravely testifies, we are free to choose in all circumstances.

When my youngest (Emma) was 7 or 8, my wife, Judy, and I began confronting her with her freedom to choose for herself, and to consider the consequences of her choices. Early on, we would have to "coach" her through the process of identifying the consequences.

When Emma would ask to do something that we felt was not likely to turn out well, we would ask her, "Emma, if you do that, what do you think will happen?" This question was intended to help her learn to connect her choices with their likely consequences (natural or applied). Next, we would ask her, "Is there anything else you could do?" And then lastly, "What do you think will happen if you make that choice instead?"

In the end, even at 7, most of the time Emma would make the productive choice. Learning to make choices by weighing the short- and longer-term consequences at a young age is a life skill that can change everything.

Regardless of how you've experienced it, accountability is not consequences, it's *ownership*. At the heart of accountability is free-will choice. You always, always, always have choice. That doesn't mean you will always like the choices available to you, but you have choice.

Our definition of accountability *as* ownership first appeared in our book *The 12 Week Year*, and was perhaps an even more disruptive insight than our view that your year should be only 12 weeks long. Our insight, which has changed the lives of so many of our readers and clients, was that the power of true accountability lies entirely in our freedom of choice.

There have been others before us who have talked about accountability as choice and have hinted at this notion of accountability as ownership. Peter Koestenbaum and Peter Block, in their profound book *Freedom and Accountability at Work: Applying Philosophic Insight to the Real World*, establish the conflict between management and the individuals they lead when it comes to who is the author of accountability.

For us, what makes our take unique is that the insights that we have had regarding personal accountability have arisen directly out of the crucible of working with others so that they can tap into their capabilities in life. In helping our clients, we have found some basic tools and approaches that cut through the fog of what you control and what you don't control, creating immense freedom along the way.

Relationships have been saved. Businesses have been transformed. Careers have been resurrected, and the world has been changed by the working model of accountability that we have built in partnership with our clients. In short, accountability is a much more powerful tool than most people realize.

In the course of our work, we have fleshed out a working model of accountability that allows our clients to take ownership of their thinking and actions in such a way that they can accomplish things that they had stopped trying to do – believing that they were just not good enough, diligent enough, or worthy enough to accomplish before. We have helped people to see their degrees of freedom and then to act on them.

In spite of the common notions about accountability, when we ran a promotion for voluntary accountability groups recently, we had the program fill up faster than any other promotion before or since. It seems that many people instinctively know that there *is* life-changing power in becoming more accountable, regardless of the negative connotations of the word. Accountability isn't an outside-in process where others force you to be accountable – it is an inside job, a personal stance in life that changes everything!

Before you start to think that this is just another book that will focus on how leaders can create more accountability in their teams, I want to be clear. A true understanding of accountability is that it is a choice and cannot be forced. In its purest form, accountability is simply taking ownership of one's actions and results.

Accountability is the foundation of lasting individual success. It enables people to reach their most important personal goals and objectives, and in the long run become more influential, more successful, and more fulfilled.

A victim allows his success to be limited by external circumstances, people, or events. As long as we continue to be victims of our circumstances, we will experience life as a struggle, and other people as a threat. Accountability, on the other hand, allows you to gain control of your life, to shape your destiny, to fulfill your potential. Accountability is not about blaming yourself, or a way to enable punishment of others. It is simply a stance in life where one acknowledges one's role in outcomes.

Accountability is not concerned with fault but, rather, what it takes to create better results. Until we and our organizations accept ownership of our actions, and our outcomes, we will be helpless to change or improve the results. Once we accept that our actions have an impact on the outcome, then, and only then, are we truly empowered to create the results we desire. Some of the more powerful benefits of accountability are highlighted in Table 1.1.

Table 1.1   The Benefits of Accountability

- *Healthy relationships.* Accountable relationships lift both people.
- *Better health.* Less stress and more control lead to greater well-being.
- *Confidence in abilities.* Track record builds an assuredness to handle what comes up.
- *Better results.* Accountability leads to better execution of the high-value actions.
- *Growth.* Accountable people push past their comfort zone more frequently.
- *Learning.* Confronting what isn't working creates learning about what does work.
- *Respect.* Results, commitment, and integrity are all hallmarks of accountability.
- *Sustained career success.* High personal effectiveness leads to more options.
- *Ability to overcome setbacks.* Accountable people aren't for long victims of circumstance.
- *Being in demand/More Opportunities.* People want you on their projects, initiatives, and teams.
- *Better finances.* Accountability in one area fosters accountability in others.
- *Greater self-assurance and confidence.* Accountable people are high in self-efficacy.
- *More control in life.* Empowered people say no to things that don't fit.
- *More influence.* Respect leads to a platform to influence others.
- *Better control of time use.* Fewer messes to clean up – don't engage in low-value work.

When we acknowledge our accountability, our focus shifts from defending our actions to learning from them. *Failures* simply become feedback in an ongoing process of becoming excellent. Unfavorable circumstances and uncooperative people don't prohibit us from reaching our goals. We stand in a different way, thereby creating different results.

Accountability is a life stance based on the understanding that you don't control circumstances and events, but you do control how you respond to them. Accountability begins with the realization that the quality of your choices determines the quality of your life.

When you view accountability as choice, as ownership, I think it is probably *the* most empowering concept to live your best life. Accountability holds the keys to unlocking most everything you want in life, from career success to income and wealth, good health, strong relationships, confidence, and personal fulfillment. Accountability doesn't guarantee these things, but it does give you your best chance at achieving them.

In our work with thousands of top performers and others pursuing greatness, we've seen time and time again how critical accountability is to success. If there is one characteristic that is a game changer, it's accountability.

In this book, we outline the key tenets of true accountability. The first half of the book focuses on individual accountability. This creates a health foundation for growth and success. In these chapters, we demystify the concept with real-life examples that will help you more fully grasp accountability and its impact. The second half of the book focuses on applying accountability as a leader. Whether you are a leader at work, in your community or place of worship, or in your home, you will discover how much of what you have learned about accountability is actually causing issues and inhibiting performance. You will learn a better way of applying accountability and why you will want to discard the practice of "holding" people accountable.

Setbacks and challenges are part of life. The key to success and happiness is how you handle the failures – and the victories. Armed with the truth about accountability, you will be better enabled to pursue opportunities as they arise and to overcome the inevitable setbacks. Ultimately, you will be empowered to achieve what you are truly capable of in life.

Greatness is a natural byproduct of accountability and cannot be attained, or sustained, without it. All truly successful people are accountable long before anyone recognizes their accomplishments. Accountability, more than any other personal character trait, ensures that you will live the best life possible in the circumstances that you face.

2

THE VICTIM MINDSET

The Power of Mindset

"Free your mind and the rest will follow."

— Foster and McElroy

Mindset is the source of everything that gets accomplished in life. The way one thinks drives behavior, and behaviors create results. Thinking is so fundamental to success that if it isn't intentional, results cannot be optimized.

At a macro level there are two mindsets with respect to accountability – either victim or accountable. In this chapter, we will unpack the victim mindset. As you will read, it's pretty grim. This chapter is not designed to discourage you but rather to increase your awareness of the detrimental and insidious nature of a victim mindset. (We promise to keep the gore to a minimum.)

There are times when success appears to be the result of luck, or having a head start in life. While inherited wealth and position can be a great boost to financial success, they are not what it takes to be successful, or to maintain success.

There are multiple news stories about everyday people getting lucky in life, winning the lottery, or receiving an unearned inheritance. Interestingly, a few years after receiving their riches there are two common, and starkly differing, winner's stories.

One frequent scenario is where recipients apply a level of personal discipline – maybe buy a new house and a few nice things – but generally manage their assets conservatively and make prudent investments and savings. They also tend to be private and don't radically change their lifestyles or spending patterns. Those are the people who keep their assets.

The other scenario is where the lottery winners indulge in an immediate spending spree – buying cars, vacations, houses – denying themselves very little. They spend without a strategy to retain and maintain their newly acquired wealth in the long run. These are the stories that don't end well, sometimes even worse than before the windfall.

The differences in behavior are driven by the mindset of the winners. People who were fiscally accountable before the new-found wealth tended to stay accountable (and wealthy). People who were not financially disciplined generally lost everything. It clearly wasn't the money that maintained success; it was the mindset. The lesson is that individual luck is not a great determinant of life success, but rather, one's way of thinking is. At its very heart, accountability, and the long-term success it creates, resides in our thinking.

IT'S ALL ABOUT YOUR THINKING

In this and the next chapter, we will compare and contrast what we call a *victim mindset* with an *accountable mindset*. We will explore how these different mindsets generate significantly different trajectories and results. Before we dig into the specifics, however, we want to introduce the model that we will use to compare and contrast these differing mindsets.

The foundation for this comparison is what we refer to as the *RAT model*. The basic premise of this model is that the results (R) we create in life are the outcomes of our actions (A). And our actions in turn arise from a broad assembly of impulses, habits, mental models, values, desires, fears, feelings, experiences, and knowledge, all of which form what we define as our thinking (T). In essence, the model implies that our underlying thinking creates our results in life.

The British statistician George E. P. Box is credited with saying, "All models are wrong, but some are useful." This is true of the RAT model as well; there are complexities to human behavior, but the model is useful in the effort to improve performance.

In our book *The 12 Week Year*, we shared a simple framework to help our readers understand our view on how people create their results. We called that framework the RAT model: R for results, A for action, and T for thinking. Thinking drives actions and actions create results. In the end, our thinking creates the results we experience in life.

The challenge we face when we want to address our thinking is that our mindsets are amorphous, dynamic, and largely unconscious. In certain situations, our thinking can shift and drive one set of actions; in other situations our thinking is completely different and generates a different set of actions. Because we are influenced every moment by our immediate environment and our internal physiological state, accordingly our actions can be somewhat inconsistent and unpredictable, but they are always an outgrowth of our underlying thinking.

Further complicating the ability to think more intentionally is that our thinking is a combination of both our unconscious beliefs and our moment-to-moment conscious thoughts. If our actions are partially the result of our unconscious beliefs, it stands to reason that it is difficult to change what we are not fully aware of.

Finally, to add yet another challenge, our thoughts can often be in conflict with one another. For example, I may simultaneously want to eat ice cream, and also want to weigh less than I currently do. This trade-off is exacerbated by the temporal nature of the benefits of the choice. The ice cream is instant gratification, while the weight loss is delayed, occurring sometime in the future.

In spite of the challenges that arise, there remain significant benefits to intentionally directing our thinking. We have found in our decades of experience helping our clients to achieve better results that when there is an execution breakdown or a struggle to achieve a certain outcome, it is almost always useful to assess the underlying thinking so that we better understand the *why* behind what we do, and thereby increase the odds that we can make the thinking shifts needed to drive productive action.

As we dig into thinking, we have an important caveat that we want to make clear. We are not psychologists. We don't dabble in psychotherapy. We don't delve into the realm of mental health, and we strongly recommend that if you feel that you need additional help regarding your thinking, you seek the aid of one of the many qualified, licensed, and trained metal health professionals out there.

To find a qualified professional near you try: https://www.ratemds.com/best-doctors/?country=us&specialty=psychologist

THE VICTIM MINDSET

If accountability, as we argued in the last chapter, is such a powerful life stance, why do so few seem to fully embrace it? That's a question that we have grappled with for years. Why do so many people seem to prefer to see themselves and to portray themselves as victims of external factors, instead of taking greater accountability for their choices and ultimately changing their lives for the better?

It is important to note that when we use the term *victim mindset* we are referring to the generalized tendency of an individual to view unfavorable circumstances and poor results as outside of their control. This is not to be confused with what psychologists refer to as the *victim syndrome* or *victim complex,* which is related to people who

(continued)

(*continued*)

have experienced real trauma that affects their view of the world.

Both Michael and I understand that there are *true* victims in life. Children who have been abused, people who have been lied to by someone they trust, victims of fraud or violence. That is not what we are referring to here. When we use the term *victim* we are referring to individuals who fall short in some way and look to avoid their accountability in the situation.

Why do so many people seem to look outside themselves when things go wrong, instead of looking inward? Why do we so often blame the external world for our shortcomings? Psychologists say that blame helps to preserve self-esteem, or in conflict, blame helps as an attempt to resolve those conflicts. Another reason that blame is so common is that blaming others and external factors is also easier than blaming yourself, because if the fault isn't yours, you never have to do the work to "fix it."

As the RAT model implies, our mindset causes us to act and react the way that we do. Whether we take a victim stance or an accountable one depends on how we think about the world, and our degrees of freedom to change it for the better.

FLAWED THINKING

We often tell our clients, "Show me your daily actions, and I can predict your future." If you want to know what your health will be like three years from now, look to your daily actions. If you want to know what your relationships will be like three years from now, look to your daily actions. If you want to know what your career and income will be three years from now, look to your daily actions.

We intuitively know that our actions create what we experience in life, but too often we attribute a greater role to external factors that are out of our control. While things often happen that affect our outcomes, the problem with attributing primary causality to those things is that if our results in life are the outcome of external forces and events, then we are powerless to significantly change our circumstances. We become stuck – we become victims to a life shaped by forces outside of our control.

Over the years, we have conducted hundreds of training workshops for leaders, professionals, and entrepreneurs. In these events, we often dig deeply into the concept of personal accountability.

What we have discovered is that the majority of our participants believe that most people are just not naturally accountable. In our discussions, attendees generally estimate that somewhere between 10 to 20 percent of the general population are personally accountable. As a result of these assumptions, nearly all of these participants are in systems that attempt to force "accountability" via consequence management.

If our clients are correct, for so many people to avoid personal accountability with all of its benefits, then the benefits of choosing the victim role must be even more attractive. When we ask attendees to identify what they think the benefits of playing the victim are, we get virtually the same responses each time. A victim stance allows people to:

- Shift blame to external circumstances or to other people.
- Avoid punishment or negative repercussions for mistakes.

- Protect one's self-image by not confronting personal mistakes and shortcomings.
- Save face with peers, managers, and customers.
- Eliminate the need for change and expend less effort by avoiding the work and time needed to get better.
- Avoid the painful effort of deep introspection needed to discover and confront the truth.
- Receive potential financial rewards or avoid financial penalties.
- Minimize workloads as others learn to ask less of me.
- Receive sympathetic attention.

In truth, that is a pretty attractive list to many people – especially the last item. In one workshop a participant stood up at the conclusion of this list exercise and exclaimed, "I'm going Victim!" After the laughs subsided, there was consensus that many of the items on the list are appealing, if not seducing. The bottom line is that there are innumerable persuasive reasons for people to avoid accountability.

Further reinforcing a victim mindset, society often supports the thinking that we are not to blame for our unfortunate circumstances. You can look at your favorite news source on any day and you will likely find stories of people blaming someone, or something, other than themselves for the situation they find themselves in. While there are certainly external factors that impact all of us negatively, when we give too much weight to external events we immediately lose effective influence over the results we achieve in life.

However, as we have said before, there are times when people are truly victims. We are not referring to those situations.

Stories we hear, and the groups we associate with, can subtly promote a victim mindset. Recent studies show that events – whether experienced firsthand or by reading about them – can affect the mindset of individuals by encouraging them to either avoid or embrace personal accountability.

In 2010, Nathanael Fast and Larissa Z. Tiedens conducted experiments to determine if blame might be contagious.[1] In one of their experiments, they asked 100 participants to read a news clip about an actual failure of a well-known politician. One group read an excerpt, including a statement in which the politician blamed special-interest groups for the failure, and a second group read a statement where he took personal responsibility for the failure.

Next, the study participants were asked to write about an unrelated personal failure with an explanation of what caused it. Something truly profound was revealed about human nature in the results. It turns out that the accountability stance of others strongly influences the way that we choose to think and act – and it happens without us being aware that it's happening!

Those who read about the politician blaming others for his failure were twice as likely (as the group that read the other version) to blame someone else for their own failures! A second experiment with a similar setup, in which participants read about a fictional failure crafted by the researchers, produced the same results.

The second experiment focused on the topic of university students who found it difficult to find a job upon graduation.

---

[1] Nathanael Fast and Larissa Z. Tiedens, Blame contagion: The automatic transmission of self-serving attributions, *Journal of Experimental Social Psychology*, 46 (2010), 97, 106, 10.1016/j.jesp.2009.10.007

In the first part of the experiment, one group read a passage where students stated that the lack of job prospects was largely because the university did not provide enough support, while a second group read about students who took responsibility for their difficulty in finding a job.

In the second part of the study, participants read about a hypothetical company and were instructed to assume the role of an employee who was involved in a project that failed, resulting in a significant financial loss for the company. They read that they (as the employee) were largely to blame for the failure, but others on the team played a role as well. They were then asked to respond to the supervisor's request to explain the failure.

Just as with the first experiment, those participants exposed to arguments blaming the university transferred more of the blame to others than did those who were exposed to the version in which the students took responsibility.

The headline here is that blame is contagious, but the good news is, so is accountability! When we see or hear stories about someone else avoiding personal accountability, we are more likely to do the same when we experience setbacks or make mistakes. When we hear stories of taking personal accountability, we tend to tell more accountable stories ourselves.

At the end of the day, avoidance of accountability comes in large part from the desire to protect one's self-image. We all want to feel good about who we are. Research has shown that all of us have a self-image protection desire. And as we see others engage in self-image protection through transference of blame and other techniques, we adopt a similar posture. Choose your associations carefully!

Not only are the benefits of playing the victim attractive, but as you can see from the research it's contagious as well. It's pretty clear *why* we choose to play the victim; the benefits are substantial. *How* we play the victim is equally interesting.

"Do I know all there is to know here, Matt?"
— Tom Cruise in *Jerry Maguire*

One way that we avoid accountability is pretending not to know certain inconvenient facts in a situation where we are invested in a certain outcome or a "story" that we desperately want to believe.

When we have a strong emotional investment in something that we want to happen, or that we want to believe about ourselves, we can easily ignore incongruent information, and warning signs that may be present, pretending to ourselves that they are not real or relevant. Later, when those situations play out differently than we had hoped, we often claim ignorance of what we were partially aware of all along.

A personal example of this occurred when I was offered and accepted an executive position at a company that I had been consulting with.

I had worked closely with the CEO prior to accepting the position, and he always acted quickly on my advice. I could tell that he valued my opinion and my work, and I was enjoying the ego boost of significantly impacting a Fortune 500 company so early in my career.

In the euphoria of this huge success, I easily ignored some disconcerting behaviors on the part of the CEO. In my consulting work prior to accepting the offer, I had seen some things that I should have recognized as the warning signs they were.

While the CEO was easy to consult for, working for him was another matter completely. He was unrealistically demanding of his executives and, simultaneously, brutally dismissive of them. In meetings, he would verbally degrade his direct reports. He clearly communicated that he didn't value their opinions, and in fact would literally ask them not to speak. I had also noticed that he churned through executives, though at the time I just wrote it off to them being "weak players." In my euphoria, I chose to ignore all those inconvenient truths and readily accepted the position when it was offered. Looking back on it today, it stands out as one of the biggest mistakes I made in my career.

Almost as soon as I started, the CEO was meddling in my role, reversing my decisions, and dismissing my ideas. The advice he had eagerly accepted when I was a consultant, he was now rejecting. I began to understand that those signs I ignored when I was offered the job were the biggest issues I was to face at the new company.

Upon my involuntary departure less than a year after accepting that position, I clung to the belief that I had been taken advantage of and lied to. And while it was true that I could argue I wasn't treated fairly, the full truth is, there were things that I pretended not to know that were almost certain to cause me to fail.

For me to see myself as a victim, and position myself that way, was all about protecting my self-image. I knew how difficult the leader was to work for and how many different executives he had rotated through before me, yet I chose to ignore all that, thinking somehow it would be different for me – pretending not to know.

REINFORCING THE VICTIM MINDSET

Another way that people can avoid accountability is by building an environment around them that reinforces their victim mindset. The most effective way to do this is to associate with others with victim mindsets. These associates rarely, if ever, challenge the victim's view of the situation – in fact, they often help to reinforce that mindset.

When we are avoiding accountability, the last thing we want is for someone to call us out. Rather, we appreciate people who will "jump on board our victim train" and provide the reinforcement and sympathy that we so desire. As a result, we seek out people who have a similar mindset to our own.

This reinforcement dynamic is a real thing – and it can be used to bolster a victim mentality (or an accountable one). Many top performers seek to associate together because accountable people help to build up other accountable people. And this dynamic is why "complainers" are drawn to other complainers. In this way, they can commiserate together with no risk of having to acknowledge their roles in the negative outcomes they experience.

The mindset of the victim is to focus on the aspects of the situation that they don't control, the things that are outside of themselves. Doing so absolves them of any responsibility for their poor results. Situations turn out badly because of things outside of their control, not because of their choices or actions.

A perfect example of this dynamic is how easy it is to blame our spouse or partner when things go awry. We are late for an important school function, and I blame my wife because she wasn't ready on time. She in turn blames me because I didn't help get the kids ready to go.

Relationship counselors will tell you that most of the couples they counsel blame each other for their own unhappiness.

We look for reasons outside ourselves and learn to ignore the deeper degrees of control that we have in situations because it lessens the sting of falling short. Deep down, we also believe that others will never become aware of the things we could have done, and chose not to do, that would have likely created a better outcome.

The problem is that although there are some benefits to playing the victim, there are also costs – long-term, sometimes life-destroying costs. We also ask participants in our sessions about what they think the costs of the victim mindset might be. And just like the list of victim benefits, the costs are usually similar every time we ask:

- Victims lose confidence in themselves and accomplish less than what they are capable of in life.
- They lose respect from others – especially those who are successful themselves.
- They lose self-respect as well because they "know" that they contributed to their failures even though they don't admit it to themselves or others.
- They repeat their mistakes since they blame things that they have no control over and therefore cannot change.
- Victims lose time – wasting days, months, and even years on being stuck instead of learning and improving. This leads to significant loss of potential income, and many fewer opportunities come their way.
- Victims accomplish less than their peers.
- Those close to people with a victim mindset learn to see through the excuses to the truth, which results in strained relationships.

In the end, people with victim mindsets perform poorly relative to their capabilities, get lower results, have worse health, experience greater lifelong stress, grow less, learn less, fail more, tap into less of what they are capable of, and have less stability than those having more accountable mindsets.

The ultimate costs of being a victim are that your relationships and performance suffer, your results are poor, and in most areas you fall short of what you are capable of.

Because victims are in the habit of blaming others, it's only a matter of time before their family and friends become scapegoats and targets to blame. It goes without saying that blaming people close to you for your inadequacies and failures has a detrimental effect on those relationships. The people who remain as friends are primarily those with similar victim mindsets.

In addition, poor results make it difficult for the victim to find any degree of sustained success and victory. The habit of not confronting *their* actions, not being willing to see the correlation between their lack of results and their behaviors, prevents them from improving and creating more favorable results in the future. Over time, these losses are compounded, ultimately leading to falling short in the most important areas of life.

Because relationships are damaged and results are poor, the victim often experiences significant potential loss of time, money, and opportunity. The time loss arises from a combination of not advancing and having to deal with the same problems and bad situations again and again. Time is wasted by working to "cover one's tracks" to absolve themselves of agency in their undesirable outcomes. Because time is an inelastic resource, the cost of the victim mindset is huge.

Financial loss is still another area where victims pay a price. I can't think of one person with sustained financial success who is not personally accountable. Of the tens of thousands of people I've met during my lifetime, from around the world and from all walks of life, I don't know one who has a victim mindset and is wealthy. I'm sure there's one somewhere out there. Perhaps they won the lottery or a big lawsuit, but the point is that most victims struggle financially. Part of why they struggle financially is that they miss out on opportunities that arise. When you encounter a promising opportunity, you likely don't think of getting someone involved who lacks accountability, struggles to get results, and has a victim mindset. In fact, that's the last person you would pick.

Think about the costs of no growth, no learning, and repeating mistakes. This is a deadly trio. Three harbingers of doom. Because the victim lacks the confidence, and will, to look deeply at their mistakes, shortcomings, and failures, there is no chance for learning or growth. Learning and growth require self-awareness and an accurate self-image. It's never easy to look at the role you played in a failure, but that is one of the fundamental ways in which we learn and grow. When we refuse to confront our shortcomings, we perpetuate those shortcomings and condemn ourselves to repeatedly experiencing the same consequences. By not learning from our mistakes, we are destined to repeat them.

As bad as all of these costs are, I think the biggest might be the loss of confidence, self-respect, and self-esteem. When you lose these healthy beliefs, it makes it difficult to succeed in life. Without confidence, you second-guess your decisions and it becomes virtually impossible to move forward with any degree of certainty. Success at any level involves some risk, which requires a certain degree of confidence to embrace. You must have enough confidence to deal with the inevitable challenges and setbacks that are part of succeeding. The victim mindset doesn't handle failure in a healthy way, and thereby avoids necessary risk.

As we've discussed, the victim looks at failure as a result of something outside of themselves in an effort to protect their psyche and image. But the very act of embracing the internal victim actually damages one's belief in oneself, making it more and more difficult to take ownership. The cycle of avoidance leading to a lack of confidence and lowered self-esteem becomes a downward spiral that ultimately culminates in failure and disappointment.

The lifetime costs of a victim mindset are numerous and staggering. The in-the-moment benefits of taking on a victim mindset pale by comparison.

The problem is that adopting a victim mindset is easy to do. The benefits (although short term) happen immediately. The prices paid for a victim mindset, on the other hand, can be lifelong and devastating, yet since they are delayed, they are often ignored in the moment. The price–payoff timing is why we hear so many victim stories in the press, the workplace, and at home.

In the next chapter, we will explore what we call the accountable mindset and compare the costs and benefits of that life stance.

3

THE
ACCOUNTABLE
MINDSET

Accountability is the fundamental driving force for sustained success in life. While a victim mindset can trap us in the mire of dissapointment, regrets, and resentment, an accountable one can set us free to achieve our biggest aspirations and live a life of meaning and fulfillment. This chapter on the mindset of accountability is the antithesis of Chapter 2.

In the last chapter, we listed some of the payoffs and prices arising from what we defined as a *victim mindset*. Overall, we argued that there is a significant negative impact on lifetime results when this mindset is nurtured and embraced. Why, then, do so many people seem to choose to embrace their internal victim?

We suggest that there are two primary reasons. The first is that being accountable also comes with some significant costs. The costs of accountability can include:

- *The need to change personally*. Discomfort arises from the work needed to grow personally, and to improve results.
- *Loss of self-image preservation*. We must let go of ego-preserving blame of other people and/or external events for our shortfalls.

- *The honest examination and confrontation of our own agency in our current situation.* This can be an immediate blow to our ego, challenge our worldview, and negatively affect our self-efficacy in the short-term.
- *The increased risks associated with acknowledging our personal culpability to others.* These risks include the potential loss of freedom, income, career, relationships, and the loss of perceived control.
- *Pushback from others in our relationship sphere who may see the world through their own victim filters.* When *we* personally confront the truth, it can become uncomfortable for others who remain invested in their own victim perspectives.
- *Spurring personal conflicts.* Being personally accountable can also create potential interpersonal conflict when the negative consequences created by our choices spill over onto others who may have had little to no role to play in the outcome themselves.
- *Looking incompetent in the short term.* There is a loss of short-term personal effectiveness as we go through the learning curves required to improve our results over the long term.
- *Loss of another potential fall guy.* We may take the entire blame for a mistake when others may have also contributed to the breakdown but are unwilling to admit it.
- *Missed pleasurable opportunities.* When we say yes to the work to get better, we almost always will have to say no to something else that we enjoy.
- *Time cost and money costs.* Being accountable can require time and/or money to do what it takes to get it right.

Those are some real prices for taking personal accountability for our shortfalls. Given those costs, choosing to take a victim stance seems more understandable. Blaming our failures or shortfalls on others or external events can insulate us from these prices in the short term.

We listed the pain of change as the first cost on our list because it is perhaps the highest and most immediate price we will pay for choosing to grow in accountability. Many people dislike the change required to grow, to get better, to step out into the required uncertainty and struggle involved with self-improvement.

The fact is that most personal change is uncomfortable and unpleasant, and we generally look to avoid it. In fact, we have a section in our first book, *The 12 Week Year,* that describes an "Emotional Cycle of Change." There is often a predictable pattern for our emotions as we experience change, and we call the emotional nadir of change, the *Valley of Despair.* Most people don't seek out that aspect of change, yet if we're to be accountable, we will need to learn to lean into change, not to lean back from it. Taking more ownership will require one to do things differently and to do different things. That means change. That means a willingness to fully embrace the changes needed for us to grow when our current mindset and approaches are not delivering.

It is human nature to seek comfort. Many people seem to place it as their ultimate value. In fact, we believe that comfort is the main desire that holds people back from accomplishing what they are truly capable of. We all like that which is familiar, enjoyable, and comes with a degree of certainty. That is why it's always easier to come home after a long day of work and just flop on the couch versus getting on the exercise bike.

But if I've taken ownership of my health and fitness, then I am obliged to choose the path of less comfort – in this case, to get on my bike, lift the weights, or go for the run. The same is true with the rest of the list of accountability costs – from risk, to exposure, to an investment in time, they all demand physical or emotional effort to overcome and grow through.

All of this brings us to the second reason that people often choose to be a victim over being accountable. It has to do with the temporal nature of the costs and benefits of each choice. If we compare the lists of prices and payoffs for victim and accountable mindsets and assess whether they are realized in the short term versus the long term, it's clear why so many choose the victim path.

If you consider the costs of being accountable, as unattractive as they are, they are paid in the short term. The discomfort, the risk, the exposure, for almost all the costs are paid immediately, and usually for a relatively short period. The majority have a half-life of hours, days, or in some cases, weeks.

In comparison, the prices of a victim mentality (as we covered in the last chapter), are long term and frequently permanent. Loss of confidence, self-respect, time, and opportunity, all have long-term prices. Repeating mistakes, continued failure, poor performance, and relationship damage are costs that may not be experienced immediately, but will certainly be experienced in the long run. These costs are real, and unless the mindset that created them changes, they are unavoidable. When you choose to see yourself as a victim in life, these outcomes are devastating. Every time we take the victim path, we are accruing one or more of these debts in the balance sheet of our life.

Conversely, the benefits of being the victim are immediate and short-lived. Things like ego protection, sympathy, and attention from others are all experienced in the moment, but they are fleeting. These are not lasting effects, but rather relatively instant and temporary. The good feelings of relief are experienced quickly, and then they are gone, and what we are left with is a long-term personal trail of carnage in our lives. Ultimately, there is no way to avoid the costs if we choose the victim approach. Sure, we will experience the benefits for a brief and fleeting period, but they are always followed by the costs, which we then often experience for a lifetime.

Even though the prices and payoffs over time are clearly in favor of being accountable, I think the desire for instant gratification explains why so many still choose to play the victim in life and avoid accountability. The costs of being accountable are experienced instantly, in the moment. There is no avoiding them – the discomfort, the risk, the humbling effect, the hit to the ego – all of these are painful and come virtually the instant we choose accountability. The benefits of accountability can be days, weeks, months, even years in the making, while the costs are front-ended.

In economics, the premium one places on enjoyment sooner versus enjoyment later is called *time preference*. The culture in the West has been shifting toward a shorter time preference for decades. This means that the payoff–price trade-off is shifting culture at large in the direction of the choice of a victim mindset.

Research shows that most people naturally optimize for the present moment (see Table 3.1). None of us look to create unpleasant moments in our life. Quite the contrary, we all look to experience comfort and joy. We want comfort, and

Table 3.1   Benefit – Cost Timings for Victim and Accountable Mindsets

	Benefits	Costs
Victim Stance	Immediate	Delayed
Accountable Stance	Delayed	Immediate

we want it now. We are strong proponents of living life in the moment, but we also know that a long-term perspective helps us to choose more efficaciously in the moment.

Smoking is a classic example. As of May 2021, the medical journal *Lancet* estimates that there are more than 1 billion smokers worldwide. Most smokers likely know that they're at a much higher risk of developing lung cancer and other debilitating diseases, and yet they continue to smoke. And even for those in areas with less access to the health statistics, shortness of breath, lack of stamina, and the high expense of cigarettes are apparent.

For those who do know the data and the risks, the threat of lung cancer is years or decades into the future (and even then it isn't 100 percent certain), but the immediate gratification of satisfying the craving for nicotine by smoking is attractive and certain.

For smokers aware of the downsides of smoking, the delayed gratification of good health later in life does not outweigh the cost of giving up the pleasure of the right now, which is available the instant they light up. This is true with many of the lifestyle choices we are confronted with daily: tasty but unhealthy foods in the moment outweigh better health in the future, lounging around beats out rigorous exercise, alcohol tonight outweighs the pain tomorrow, in-the-moment impulse spending feels better than frugality, and so on. The probabilities of the future costs may be considered, but they are often rationalized away with a half-hearted intention to start being better tomorrow – after all, there is plenty of time to get on track later.

This is what makes choosing accountability so rare. This is why so few people keep their New Year's resolutions. The trade-off of immediate gratification versus future cost, combined with our innate desire for comfort, drives most behavior patterns.

If I'm optimizing for the moment, striving to create comfort and pleasure, the accountable choice is not very attractive. In today's ever-shortening, time-preference society, this issue seems to me to be more pronounced every year. Increasingly, our focus is on right now.

My wife, Judy, says that one of her favorite advertising taglines ever was "Life is short, buy the shoes." And I can testify that she lives by that motto! Buying the shoes is fine – if you can afford it. However, too many people make poor financial decisions in the moment based on the immediate benefits and delayed costs. Then down the road, when they don't have the necessary resources to pay their bills or to fund their retirement, they can often have a strong temptation to blame the "system" – sometimes even expecting others to pay for their poor decisions.

This lack of ownership of our choices and the consequences they create happens every day in ways big and small. We intentionally ignore the long-term effects of our choices for the feel good in the moment. Then later, when confronted with the costs of those decisions, we frequently attempt to absolve ourselves from any accountability, and we can even frame ourselves as a victim of circumstances, or other people, when in reality it was our own poor choices that led to the current state of affairs.

All of us at times struggle to be accountable; it's not easy. Clearly, no one has a fully accountable, or fully victim, mindset. We all live on a continuum somewhere between the two polar opposites. Often, we are more accountable in some areas and not so much in other areas. The good news is that as we become more aware of where we lack accountability, and then act on that awareness, we can move more toward the accountable end of the scale through better choices.

An interesting thing happens when we start to adopt a more accountable mindset. Just as present victim thinking increases future victim thinking, present accountability thinking increases future accountability thinking. Both mindsets tend to reinforce themselves.

In general, accountable people are also successful people, and those with a predominately victim mindset tend to struggle with creating lasting success in life. Ironically, those initially seeking to optimize their short-term comfort often create lives of long-term discomfort, frustration, and stress, and those willing to sacrifice their comfort in the short term live lives of long-term joy and success.

Choosing to be accountable is not easy. In fact, it can be downright hard. In the end, though, the benefits of being accountable are all the things we long for in life – confidence, esteem, success, fulfilling relationships, and so on. You will never fully experience what you are truly capable of without a high degree of personal accountability. It is a foundational building block for success, impact, and meaning in life.

As we discussed in Chapter 2, the results we achieve in life arise from our actions, and our actions are driven by our thinking. To build more, to create more, to expand your impact, you must work on your thinking. Specifically, you must become even more accountable for, and take greater ownership of, your own thinking.

One of the first places that thinking can limit what we are accountable for is in our beliefs about what we are capable of. Henry Ford said it best: "If you think you can, or you think you can't, you're right." Henry knew that if you expand what you *think* you are capable of, your results will expand proportionally.

WHAT IF?

Thinking is the starting point for all great accomplishments. That is why it is critical that you are accountable at both the action and thinking level. Before you can *do* something, you must first *believe* that you can do it. To move from the *impossible* to the *given,* you must take ownership of your thinking with respect to your potential and what you are capable of creating.

The first challenge is to confront the limits of your own thinking. Ignore the reasons why you can't do something and think about what would be some amazing outcomes in your life if you could do it. What if you could make that "impossible" thing happen? What would be different for you, for your family, your friends, you community, your place of worship, even the world?

What if Elon Musk had thought that creating a car company, a space travel enterprise, an underground transportation system, and a new way of supplying the electrical grid with power were impossible? Most people would think that any one of those four things would be impossible, let alone tackling all of them simultaneously. Granted, Elon is a visionary and thinks differently than most people, and executes like crazy, but if he had thought his vision was impossible at the start, we wouldn't know his name.

All you control in life is the way that you think and the way that you act, but those two things are all you need to change your world. Believing you can do something isn't the same as doing it, but it is a necessary prerequisite.

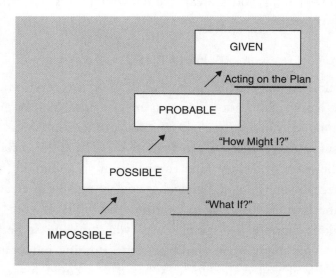

When something you want to create seems impossible to you, there are two questions to ask, in sequence, that help to break through your limited thinking and expand what you can be accountable for in life. We've already mentioned the first one: *What if?* By asking "what if?"– by considering what could be different for you and others if you could make it happen – you begin to create an emotional connection to the outcomes that you could achieve if you could do the "impossible," and once – having opened the door a crack – your thinking automatically begins to shift from "impossible" to "possible." The what-if question is the *visioning* question.

The next question that moves you from "possible" to "probable" thinking is to ask, How might I do it? But be careful: If you ask "how" too soon, before you have a strong desire to achieve your vision, you will realize you don't know how and will likely abandon your nascent dream. The *how* question is the *planning* question.

Closing the gap between where you are now and your vision is working through a series of problems and scenarios and identifying the actions needed to overcome them. Those actions become the tactics in your plan. Once you have a plan, a way to accomplish what you seek, your thinking automatically shifts from possible to probable. You have a solution to "how," and your thinking opens up even more.

A third thinking shift occurs not by asking a question but by taking action on your plan: Taking action creates momentum, answers questions, deepens your understanding, encourages you, creates results, and generates learning. When you take action and start to see progress, your thinking gradually shifts again from it's "probable" to it's a "given."

The fact is that you are first limited by your thinking about what's possible for you long before you encounter your real boundaries. But if you take the steps to shift your thinking, you can start imagining the possibilities and envisioning that you *can* accomplish what you set your mind to.

Yes, there are real boundaries. I won't win an Olympic gold medal in the downhill, I won't receive the Nobel Prize in physics, I can't be 21 again, and so on. However, I can enter a senior ski league, I can take online courses in physics, and I can get in the best shape I can be at my current age.

Accountable Relationships

A second area in which we significantly limit our thinking about what is possible is in our relationships with others. Table 3.2 compares the differences between victim and ownership mindsets in the context of people groups in our relationship sphere.

The good news is that in reality, we virtually always have meaningful influence over our results in life regardless of others. The results we create in life are generated by two things that are under our moment-by-moment control: our thinking and our actions. Our thoughts drive our actions, and our actions create our results. In the end, our thinking sets the upper and lower limits for what we will accomplish with others, much more than barriers in the external world.

To be sure, there are people who truly get in our way, things that set us back and affect our results, things that we wish were different. The problem is that if we see those "externals" as determinants, not merely influencers of our results, we are powerless to change our circumstances. To be accountable for our results, to create what we are truly capable of in life, the only approach that works is to first take ownership of our thinking. The question is this: Do we want to be right, or do we want to optimize

Table 3.2 Victim versus Ownership Mindsets

People Groups	Victim Mindset	Ownership Mindset
Co-workers	I *would* work more diligently but they don't do their fair share, so why should I? (This is a powerless position, as my career is limited by my thoughts about people whom I don't control.)	All I control is what I do. I can't worry about what they are doing, I can do my best regardless of how they behave. (This level of thinking has the power to optimize my results on my team, and in the future.)
Authorities in our lives	All they care about is what's good for them. I work harder and they make more money. Why should I expend the effort?	I can win while my boss is winning, and, if necessary, I can find a better place to work.
Successful people we know	They got lucky. They had the right connections, they started with advantages, they know the right people, they cheated. They don't deserve their success. (My resentment can sidetrack me from what's possible for me.)	I don't know what made them successful, but I control *my* thinking and actions, and those are what make me successful.
Personal relationships/peers	They aren't fair to me, they don't appreciate me, they take advantage of me, they don't contribute fairly, they blame me for everything. They don't see their own accountability in matters. (This blame mentality absolves me of the need to change my actions, and those actions are the very thing that has power to change my circumstances.)	I don't control others, but if I want to improve a relationship, I can take positive actions regardless of how they behave. If I do my best and the relationship doesn't improve, I can choose to stop investing and move on, or accept what is and stop grinding.

our results and fulfillment regardless of the barriers we face that are outside of our control?

A benefit of starting with our *internal* accountability is that it ensures that we are able to see and act on the *external* degrees of freedom that we possess. The way we think about accountability affects the way that we first perceive and then choose to act on the opportunities we have.

People with an accountable mindset handle life's challenges and setbacks differently from those without that mindset. At this point, it may help to visualize what accountability looks like in action. We all know people who have high degrees of personal accountability – people whom we respect and admire for their accomplishments and their demeanor.

What describes that person? What makes them stand out to you? People who are accountable tend to inspire trust. They are reliable, productive, successful, and confident.

Accountable people approach work differently. When faced with adversity, or when something goes awry, they don't focus on the problem and look for excuses; they tend to be solution oriented. They have a positive impact on those they work with, on the teams to which they belong. In the end, accountable people get better results.

On the other hand, at times, they also make certain people uncomfortable. They are not very tolerant of excuse makers and those who avoid accountability. In fact, they typically don't associate with people who have a victim mindset and those who are ruled by circumstances. They like people like themselves who are accountable and productive.

Now consider how their thinking is different. When they encounter friction or barriers, how do they process them mentally? The accountable mindset doesn't see problems as insurmountable or as an excuse to give up. Rather, they see the choices that are possible – the alternative approaches or solutions. They take ownership of the issues and the responsibility to find a workable solution. People with an accountable mindset are not perfect by any means. They are, however, best positioned to create positive results for themselves and those around them.

The ultimate purpose of this chapter is to help you become more aware of the current limits to your accountability mindset and to identify any areas that you want to grow in. Simply by becoming conscious of areas where you could be better, your thinking will begin to shift.

4

HOLDING
OURSELVES
ACCOUNTABLE

The driving forces behind accountability are the choices we make moment by moment. Our choice of actions creates the results we experience in life. Our choices, therefore, are best evaluated in the context of our intentions. In other words, are our choices aligned with our most important intentions? Ultimately, to become more accountable in the external elements of your life, you must first become more accountable for *what* you think about and *how* you think about those things.

As we explore the process of holding ourselves accountable, we will talk about doing so first at the thinking level. Accountability starts with our thinking, is manifested in our choices and actions, and ultimately is realized in our results. Since our thinking is the fundamental source of the results we achieve, the obvious first place to take greater ownership is in our thinking. Perhaps counterintuitively, the easiest way to identify and understand your thinking is to start by assessing your results and work backward through your actions and then ultimately into the thinking that created them.

As we pointed out in the previous chapter, it is unwise, not to mention impossible, to try to be accountable for *everything* that happens to you in life. It is important, however, to be aware of your accountability (or lack thereof) in key areas of your life that are either productive and fulfilling or stress-filled and disappointing.

Later in this chapter, we will look at some common life intentions that many of us hold, and how to think through their implications for you. We will start with a generalized *approach or process* to uncover and confront the beliefs and mindsets that you hold that are not aligned with your highest intentions – in other words, the *process* of holding yourself accountable *internally*.

The process starts with the results – identifying a result that matters to you. It might be your income, your health, your marriage, or relationships. It could be something less specific, such as that you want to be more trusting, or less judgmental. Any area where you feel there is a gap between your current results and your desired results is fair game.

The next step is to identify the actions that are creating your current results relative to the results you intended, *and* then identify the actions that you have *not* taken, or have not taken effectively, that you think would have helped you to accomplish your objective. I find that it is useful to use mind-mapping to do this so as to avoid skipping over some root causes that you are not fully conscious of and that you might otherwise miss.

INTENTIONS: LET YOUR YES BE YES

Saying *yes* to one thing usually also means saying *no* to something else. Once you have identified the set of actions that are creating your current results, it's time to dig into the thinking that drives those actions.

As you dig into the thinking that keeps you from your stated intention, start by identifying any other intentions that you have (conscious or unconscious) that might be in conflict with your stated intention.

For example, if your stated intention is to lose weight, you might also have an unstated intention to eat tasty food for comfort or pleasure. Those two intentions, if unresolved, can keep you stuck in a constant state of frustration. If the intentions are mutually exclusive, pick one. If they can both be pursued, then consciously modify the intentions you have. For example, you could take longer to get to your ideal weight and have a specified day of the week when you eat whatever sounds good – whether lasagna or ice cream, or anything else you may desire. Or, you might decide to sacrifice your food-based desire in a fully focused approach to your weight loss.

Take some time to mind map all of the intentions that you can think of that might be diffusing your efforts to reach your stated intention. For example, if you have a contentious relationship, you might have an unconscious intention that you want to be "right" in that relationship, and that might cause you to ignore some important things that you could do (or stop doing) to improve the relationship. Again, an honest friend who can speak the truth to you can be an excellent sounding board and source of deep insights into your true intentions and where they are in conflict.

If your intentions cannot be effectively pursued together (maybe you do have to give up that ice cream), then pick the one that you are most committed to. There will be a cost to pay when you consciously give up a desired intention, but the divergent-intention conflict will evaporate and you will likely be less frustrated.

One of the breakdowns when we are not achieving our intentions in life is that the beliefs that we hold, that drive our daily actions and our results in life, may or may not actually be "true." When our beliefs that impact the core behaviors driving our results are not correct, then those inaccurate or unproductive beliefs can be costly. If we don't take accountability for these key beliefs, we will significantly limit what we accomplish in life.

An example of a belief that wasn't necessarily "true" significantly impacted the results of one of our coaching clients. Jane, a wholesale rep in the financial services market, offers financial products to insurance agents needing solutions for their clients. She is experienced and is trusted by the agents that she works with. Her fundamental improvement opportunity (intention) was her sales productivity. She had good sales activity, but her closing ratio was low.

In a coaching conversation she walked us through her sales process. Everything seemed solid, except for one thing. She didn't like to ask for the close. She felt uncomfortable asking the prospect to buy. Jane's initial belief was that asking for the close increased the odds that they would say no. If she didn't ask, they might eventually reach out to her and ask her for her product, and the sale would be made.

Ironically, by acting on her belief, by *not* asking, she was effectively getting told *no* a lot. In fact, she was getting *no* at a much higher rate than the other reps in her industry. Her peers were simply asking the client to purchase, and as a result had a higher closing ratio than Jane. In the end, she created the very thing that she was trying to avoid (the *no*) by *not* asking.

We asked her if there were other ways to think about the outcomes of asking for the close. Instead of thinking that asking created the *no*, we asked her to consider the possibility that it was *not* asking that created the *no*. Perhaps the polar-opposite could be true: that if she asked, they were more likely to say *yes*. She agreed that it was possible and committed to asking for the close from everyone she had proposed product to.

Almost immediately after thinking differently about the ask, and acting based on her new thinking, her sales jumped, and she hit her annual target by the middle of September. She wasn't working any harder; she just took intentional accountability for her thinking, and her results took off.

Is there thinking that is holding you back from accomplishing your important intentions? On the most important goals that you have, are the key actions difficult for you to execute? If you know how to take the action, but you are avoiding it, ask yourself: What thinking is getting in my way?

Once you have identified your limiting thought, consider what the polar-opposite thought would be. For example, if you think that by asking for referrals you might negatively affect the relationship, the polar-opposite thinking might be that by asking for referrals, you will strengthen the relationship. Then look for evidence of how the polar-opposite thought *might* be true. The next step is to take an action that aligns with the new thought, knowing that the first few times you act will be uncomfortable.

MOVE OUT OF YOUR COMFORT ZONE

Another barrier to success lies in the way that we think about failure. It's a natural desire for most people to want to avoid failure. The problem with failure arises when we begin to fear it. Failure is a necessary part of success. If you don't fail, you are not stretching, and you are not getting better. Fear of failure turns into fear of action.

In this section, we will dig into the fear of failure that keeps so many people trapped in self-imposed mediocrity. Contrary to what many believe, failure can be positive if you leverage it well. Failure is always part of the success journey. Failure creates learning, and learning leads to improvement. Over time, consistent improvement leads to success. Even the greatest fears can be overcome by action.

Consider the story of comedian Kevin Schwartz.[1]

Kevin has agoraphobia, and for years he struggled just to leave his home. Over time, working with a psychiatrist (whom he had to visit), and receiving proper medication, he has made significant progress. His psychiatrist challenged him to "go somewhere adventurous," and he decided to visit a nearby comedy club in Madison, Wisconsin.

He had always liked writing jokes, and as he attended the club, he began to focus on writing his one-liners. Eventually, he started telling those jokes from the stage. Then, after enough practice, he auditioned for *America's Got Talent*.

On national television, before a live audience of thousands, with a panel of four judges that included Simon Cowell, Kevin stood alone on stage and delivered his routine. When he finished, he received a standing ovation from the crowd, and all of the judges voted *yes*!

(continued)

---

[1] Gabriella Rusk, www.nbc15.com, Jun 12, 2019.

(*continued*)

What Kevin did was to venture *way* outside of his comfort zone, and by doing so he accomplished more than most of us without agoraphobia ever will. He didn't feel like doing it, and admitted it was the hardest thing that he ever *chose* to do. But he did it anyway.

Most of us never push that far outside of our comfort zones. Yet, as his story makes clear, in the beginning Kevin was continually taking small step after small step toward his bigger goal of overcoming his fear and living his life.

Kevin does not want his story to be used as a weapon against other people with conditions like his. However, his story *is* an inspiration for anyone confronting fears that keep them from achieving what they are truly capable of in life.

The first step is to think about the fears that we have that are holding us back. Not all fears are equally important, just the ones that get in the way of our intentions. For example, Michael is seriously afraid of sharks. On a flight we shared together he mentioned to me that when the crew explains how to use the vests in the unlikely event of a water landing, he is not worried about surviving the crash; he's more afraid that there will be sharks in the water if he does!

Although Mike is seriously afraid of sharks, his fear doesn't limit him in any meaningful way (other than he misses out on *Shark Week*). His results in life are not significantly limited by his shark phobia.

On the other hand, if he were a marine biologist, his fear would limit his options and his success considerably. In that scenario, he might need to get over his phobia, find a new profession, or specialize in fresh-water research.

Below is a graphic of the "Zone of Comfort" that we will use to demonstrate how you can take ownership of the fears that are holding you back.

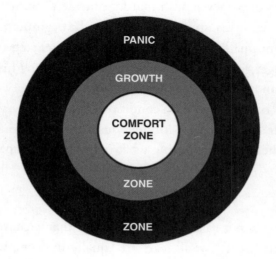

Staying in the comfort zone, where you avoid your areas of incompetency and fear, is a no-growth strategy. You don't experience discomfort, but you don't experience growth, either. Accountability for achieving what you are capable of, and what you want to achieve in life, requires you to grow and develop a healthy disregard for your comfort.

A word of caution: You can go too far if you decide to just jump off the deep end too soon. The growth zone represents moderate expansion outside of the areas you are comfortable in. This might be represented by Kevin's first foray into a local comedy club to observe the action. He was certainly uncomfortable, but he wasn't panicked. In the growth zone, learning is required but the level of learning builds on what I already know and is a reasonable stretch that allows me to learn a limited number of new things at a time. Kevin observed others and what they did to succeed, and he also wrote potential jokes for himself that he could try out when he was ready to get up on stage.

In the panic zone, learning is nearly impossible. You get confused by what it takes to succeed, and there are too many simultaneous, and steep, learning curves for us to figure it out in the moment. In the panic zone it can become so stressful that we never try to grow in that direction again. The panic zone often reinforces our worst fears. It would be like Mike jumping into a white shark feeding scrum off the coast of South Africa.

Learning how to stay in the growth zone for the areas that are important for your success is one of the most accountable things that you can do in life, and if you stick with it, you will tap into what you are truly capable of.

As you begin to understand accountability as choice, as ownership, it causes you to look at your life with new perspective. Accountability is perhaps the most powerful concept you have to live the life you desire. When you realize that your choices are the primary determinants of your current situation and your ultimate destiny, it can be exciting and sobering all at the same time.

It's a lot easier when you are struggling, or have experienced a disappointment, to look for someone or something outside of yourself as the cause of your pain and discomfort. It takes courage to look at the role you played in the creation of the outcomes that you are experiencing. But only by looking inward do we grow and become our authentic self. If we continue to focus on areas outside our control, we condemn ourselves to a life of frustration and mediocrity because, as we've discussed, we don't learn, we don't change, we don't grow.

Let's be clear: Accountability is not about blame – either external, or internal. We are not talking about looking at your choices and your actions so you can blame yourself for your failings. That is just as unproductive as blaming someone else, and often more damaging. But something almost magical happens when you willingly take ownership of the situation. There is a sense of control and empowerment that comes when you do that. You recognize you are no longer slave to your circumstances, but in fact have the ability to alter the present and shape the future.

A warning may be in order, and that is this: It doesn't always feel good in the moment. The control and empowerment don't happen immediately. What often is experienced in the moment can be very unpleasant; however, it typically lasts only a moment or two.

Accountability is *the* principle that allows you to design your life and live it on your terms.

In order to live a life of abundance and happiness, you need to look at the choices you are making in critical areas of your life, and take greater ownership going forward.

Let's look at a few key areas, starting with your health.

HEALTH

A few facts to consider:

- 32.5 percent of Americans are overweight.
- Another 36.5 percent are obese (30 lbs. or more).
- 30 million are diagnosed each year with heart disease.
- 35 million are on statins to lower their cholesterol.
- Approximately 32 million have type 2 diabetes.
- 100 million have high blood pressure.

What is most interesting is that the CDC estimates that 90 percent of type 2 diabetes, 80 percent of heart disease, 70 percent of stroke, and 70 percent of colon cancer are preventable through better lifestyle choices.

Health is one of those areas that affects every other area. Both my wife, Judy, and I are cancer survivors. And I can tell you firsthand that its extremely difficult to live your best life when you have chronic health issues. Too many people rely on drugs rather than making different choices. It's so much easier to just pop a pill each morning than it is to exercise and eat healthy. You've heard the message, *better living through chemistry*. I'm not trash talking medications and treatments – many are life-savers. The problem is that all medications have adverse side effects, some of which can be as bad as or worse than the problem they are designed to treat. The list of side effects at the end of the advertisement is alarming – depression drugs that can cause feelings of suicide. Really! Seems to me that that is exactly why you are on the drug to begin with.

The numbers don't lie. We all have the ability to lower our risk of disease and death simply through better lifestyle choices.

Taking ownership of your health and doing everything you can to be healthy and vibrant will lead to a more fulfilling life.

As a family, every morning we take wheatgrass and fish oil. Wheatgrass is considered a superfood. It is packed with vitamins and nutrients and is deemed one of the most potent foods on the planet. It has antioxidant, antibacterial, and anti-inflammatory properties. It is also highly alkaline. Cod liver oil is an omega 3 fat and contributes to a healthy heart and brain, hormonal balance, and decreased inflammation. It helps to improve cellular function, energy, mood, and aids in weight loss. In addition, we take spirulina/chlorella, an algae that is super high in chlorophyll and helps build the immune system. I have added a link at the end of this chapter if you would like to learn more about my superfoods regimen.

While we didn't make choices to intentionally get cancer, some of our choices certainly increased our odds of getting it. That's why we made the decision to make these new choices. They give us our best shot that we are aware of at staying cancer free. We can't change the past, but we can affect the future, and that's what we choose to do.

Poor health affects virtually every other area of our lives. The point is that there is a lot you can do to ensure a healthy, active life when you take ownership.

What about you and your health? What degree of ownership have you taken in this vitally important area?

CAREER

Another critical area to take greater accountability is in your work life, your career.

According to PEW Research, slightly less than half of American workers, 49 percent of them, report that they are satisfied with their jobs. Even more concerning is a recent Gallup poll that found that 85 percent of the nearly 1 billion workers worldwide are not engaged with their work – meaning they feel no real connection to their work and thus often deliver the bare minimum to get by. The US is slightly better, with approximately 70 percent disengaged, but with 16 percent of that group identified as "actively disengaged," resenting their jobs and negatively impacting the overall morale of the company.

The average American works approximately 44 to 47 hours per week, with 30 percent working 50 or more hours each week.[2] Nearly all of us spend more time working than we spend with family, friends, and other personal pursuits. For far too many people, this means that a huge chunk of their life is spent doing something that they clearly are not passionate about and don't find fulfilling. I know people, and I'm sure you do too, who are simply putting in the time looking forward to the day they can retire – 40 years of misery for 15 years of relative enjoyment.

I realize that there are aspects of any job that we find unpleasant, but the question is: Have you chosen a career that excites and stimulates you? There are some common characteristics of those who love their jobs. How do you stack up?

First, for those who love their jobs, the work is meaningful, and the job is challenging. In addition, they feel connected to the company – the cause, the vision, the impact. There is mutual respect between their boss and coworkers. And finally,

---

[2] Bureau of Labor Statistics.

they feel valued and appreciated. That sounds great, so why do so many stay in jobs that are not a great fit for them?

With so many disengaged and unsatisfied with their work, there is an obvious lack of accountability when it comes to career and job choices. It's easy to stay in a job that is unfulfilling and rationalize it. However, when you continue in a job that you don't find stimulating, you ultimately can feel trapped, which often devolves into a victim mindset. In the end, continuing in a job you don't enjoy can crush your soul.

It's never too late to take ownership of your career, and your job. Start where you stand. What can you do in your current job to make it more rewarding and fulfilling? What would change if every day you showed up with your best? In what ways can you make others feel appreciated and valued? Where can you have a bigger impact? The vast majority of people who love their jobs didn't just fall into their "dream job." They simply made the job they have more rewarding. Choose to make your job a dream job, or at least find elements that you can love until you find something you can fully embrace.

Michael has had a variety of jobs over his lifetime. Here are a few:

- He fought forest fires one summer in Kaniksu National Forest.
- In his freshman year, he took a job expressing eggs (to be used for bait) from dead fish that were deemed "too toxic to eat."
- He has planted, sheared, cut, bundled, and loaded Christmas trees onto trains.
- He has mucked horse stalls, and fed and watered horses in the bleak, mid-winter cold of northern Michigan.

- He worked hydro-blasting powerplants, automotive paint booths, and sewage plants in Detroit.
- He has worked as a teller, short-order cook, mail-room clerk, busboy, cherry picker (really – not kidding), and shelved books in a university library.

More recently he has tried his hand at being a business owner, consultant, and author.

Michael was not crazy about any of these jobs, but they all served a purpose at the time. In each, there were downsides (some bigger than others), some successes, and some failures too, but he says that he learned to focus on the work itself, controlling the things that he could, and taking satisfaction in elements of each job.

In the end, all of these experiences shaped him and were learning experiences that he still leverages to this day. Many of them he would not go back to (especially the fish and the sewage), but he is glad that he had each of them for a season.

In fact, research shows that both people who seek a good initial fit, where passion is an outcome of the job itself, and those who believe that enjoyment can be developed in a job by cultivating passion gradually over time can be just as effective in the long term at realizing passion in their work.[3]

FINANCES

Another key area in which to leverage accountability is your finances.

---

[3] Patricia Chen, Phoebe Ellsworth, and Norbert Schwarz, "Finding a Fit or Developing It: Implicit Theories About Achieving Passion for Work," *Personality and Social Psychology Bulletin* 41, no. 10 (2015): 1411–1424.

Having had times in my life when I've had lots of money, and times with very little, I can attest that having money is a good thing.

We are blessed with a group of close friends, about six couples, that we do life with. Interestingly, with each of these couples one tends to be a spender and one a saver. Unfortunately for Judy and me, we are both spenders. That can be a recipe for disaster, and we've had our share of financial disasters. When I look back, the times when I've lacked money have always been because of poor choices. They are times when we didn't have an emergency fund, we didn't save on a regular basis, and we made some bad spending decisions. In the end, we paid a big price for what is truly a lack of accountability for our finances.

The year 2009 was one of those times.

I'm from the era that predates movies on demand. We didn't even have VCRs or DVDs. When I was a kid, you had to either see it on TV or at the movies. And what was considered scary is benign by today's standards – but back then it was SCARY!

We didn't have zombies, or Dementors, we didn't even have video games where you can rip someone's spine out and stuff it down their throat – it was before all that healthy desensitization of violence that exists today.

In my day, we had the Loch Ness Monster, the Swamp Thing, and the Bermuda Triangle. But the scariest of all – at least for a 7- or 8-year-old – were those flying monkeys in *The Wizard of Oz*.

You laugh, but those things were scary. They would swoop out of the sky and tear you apart. There was no way to get away – you could try and run but they could fly and jump and run – you didn't stand a chance.

Decades later, I found myself in the middle of hell. My business, like many at the time, had taken a huge hit due to the economy, and we were also experiencing a series of other unfortunate factors. We had gone from a thriving business to barely hanging on.

If you've ever been through this, you know that it starts out kind of slow and then picks up speed. Hemingway, in his book *The Sun Also Rises*, states there are two ways you go bankrupt, "Gradually, then suddenly."

Personally, Judy and I had to tap our savings to stay afloat, and at this point in the adventure we had run out. We were scrambling to keep the business afloat and somehow keep the creditors at bay. It was an incredibly stressful time.

I knew things were going downhill fast the night the monkeys came, in the form of some repo guys in a giant tow truck.

I recall being sound asleep and suddenly waking up to a ruckus outside in our driveway. Judy got up and pulled back the curtain and exclaimed, "They're here! The monkeys are here, and they're taking your car!" Instantly, I felt like that scared 7-year-old all over again.

That was just the beginning; not too long after that, the monkeys came and took our home, then our savings. We had to sell off things in a garage sale just to have some cash to live on. When it was all said and done, we had lost everything – our cars, our home, our savings. And if that wasn't bad enough, we owed the IRS $120,000.

Now, I hope you've never experienced this and never do. I've never had anything so embarrassing and humiliating in my life. It's like those bank monkeys were mocking me.

Think about this and what I do for a living – I help others succeed. I help others make more money and have more success. And here I am, losing everything I had. That is like an Olympic swimmer drowning in a bathtub. It's like those bank monkeys were tearing me apart, just like they did the scarecrow. They tore out my confidence and threw it over there. They ripped out my self-esteem and tossed it over here. They trampled my pride and set on fire all that I had created.

It would have been easy to be a victim. After all, practically every business was affected by the recession, and many folded.

But here's the thing – no matter how scary those monkeys were or how many of them there were, I realized that they could tear my world apart, but they couldn't touch my family or my faith. And as bad as it was, the only way they could steal my hope was if I gave it to them – and I'd be damned if I was going to do that!

Michael and I got busy reinventing our business. We made massive and difficult changes. Not all of them worked. At times, it was messy and very uncertain. There were no guarantees that we would succeed. But we focused on the things we could control.

In less than 36 months, I went from no income, no savings, my car being repossessed, my house being foreclosed on, and owing over $120,000 in past-due taxes, to my personal income at an all-time high. Take that, monkeys!

Today, Judy and I have an emergency fund, savings, and investments, and we control our spending.

According to Nielsen data and the American Payroll Association, 78 percent of Americans live paycheck to paycheck, having just enough to pay their bills each month.

One of the subjects that couples argue most about is money. And even if you're not in a relationship, money affects so many aspects of your daily life. That is why it is important that you take ownership for your personal finances. People who have taken ownership report less worry and less stress, and a greater sense of peace.

RELATIONSHIPS

Relationships are another critical area to look at.

When I was newly married, I had heard that a good marriage was 50/50. That made sense to me. Each person was responsible for their half. The problem was that when I actually applied it in my marriage, it didn't work. I felt like I was giving my 50 percent, but Judy wasn't. Turns out, she felt the same. Because I felt that way, I started to pull back, and Judy did the same. Soon, we had a 20/20 marriage – which, for the record, is not ideal.

Then one Sunday morning, I was sitting in church, and I heard my pastor say that my marriage was 100 percent my responsibility. It was probably on Father's Day. On Mother's Day they (pastors) always praise the moms (and, might I add, rightly so), but on Father's Day, they talk directly to the dads about how they're screwing up.

Anyway, that wasn't easy for me to hear, and at first, I resisted it. It didn't feel fair. After all, I thought I was fine. I just needed Judy to shape up. But the more I thought about it, the more it made sense. If I took total ownership of my marriage, it couldn't guarantee I'd have a great marriage, because there is another person involved who has her own free-will choice, but it would guarantee that I'd have my best chance of having a great marriage.

Now I can be kind of slow at times, and it took me years to realize that all my relationships are 100 percent my responsibility – the good, the bad, the ugly. Realizing this has made me a lot more intentional about all my relationships.

It's just so easy to look outside of yourself and focus on what the other person could do. But you don't control that person. The only person you control is you – and at times, it feels like that's a stretch. When you are waiting and hoping that the other person will change, you are giving away your power to affect the situation and the relationship. If you stand different in the relationship, then the relationship changes. Again, it may or may not produce the specific changes you are looking for, but it will change it.

Being a dad is one of the biggest blessings in my life. I have two beautiful daughters whom I adore. I know Michael feels the same about his five children (two boys and three girls). I really appreciate having a close, loving relationship with both my girls. I can't imagine how awful it would be if we weren't close. Yet, I meet people all the time who have very strained relationships with their children, and it breaks my heart.

Johnny Carson, the famous late-night talk-show host, was incredibly successful. He was referred to as the "King of Late Night." His farewell show in 1992 drew 50 million viewers. He managed his career brilliantly and leveraged key relationships throughout his 40-plus years on TV. His business was all about relationships, and he seemed to be expert at it. He knew everyone in Hollywood and was highly respected and liked by all. Yet he was married four times and divorced three. In addition, he had very little relationship with his three sons, and what he did have was damaged. From what I've read, it appears that he blamed his exes and his kids. In the end, it was reported that he died alone with no one by his side. As successful as Johnny was in business, he obviously did not take the same degree of ownership in his personal relationships.

Think about the Top Ten people in your life – the people who matter the most to you. On a scale from 1 to 10 (1 being poor, 10 being great), rate each of those relationships. Do they look the way you want? Are they strong, healthy relationships? And what can you do to maintain those that you rate strong, and improve those that are less than what you would like? Identify one or two things you can do over the next 12 weeks for each relationship on your Top Ten list.

This is how you take ownership of the key relationship in your life. If these people matter, then it's important to take stock periodically, and be intentional about building and maintaining close, fulfilling relationships.

There are other areas that you may want to look into in addition to your health, finances, and relationships that can affect your happiness and fulfillment. Areas like your mind and emotions, your social life, intellectual pursuits, recreation and hobbies, and your spiritual life.

Typically, when you find an area that is unfulfilling or less than desirable, you will also find a lack of ownership on your part. The simple act of owning an area puts into motion a new set of actions and commitments that will bring about substantive change.

If it's important to you in life, then own it!

RESOURCES:

To learn more about superfoods I discussed earlier in this chapter, reach out to my friend, Chris Johnson, at www .ontargetliving.com.

5

LIMITS TO
HEALTHY
ACCOUNTABILITY

Often at this point a question regarding the scope of accountability comes up. The question is: "Can you be accountable for everything that happens to you?"

And the snap answer is, of course, you can. If not you, then who? It's your life. They're your choices. You create your situations and experiences. It is absolutely your accountability. Every situation, every experience, every moment of the day, for every day of your life. Yes, even that time with your ex-partner, and that situation with your co-worker. Or that time you were involved in that auto accident. It doesn't matter that the police report cited the other driver was at fault; it's still your accountability. You chose to take that route, at that time of the day.

I hope you can see how ridiculous this notion is. The truth is you are *not* accountable for everything that happens in your life, and you shouldn't try to be.

There are many experiences in your life that you have had no role in creating – they just happened to you. The notion that you are accountable for everything that happens to you is not only untrue, it's also unhealthy. Things happen to all of us in life over which we have no control and did absolutely nothing to contribute to them happening.

The misconception that you can be accountable for everything that happens in your life leads to self-blame and unproductive, debilitating guilt. Because you don't control circumstances or others, you cannot possibly be accountable for all that happens to you. When you extend accountability beyond its natural and productive scope, it can easily degrade into blaming and faulting yourself for any and all undesirable outcomes you experience.

You could be walking down the street and get hit by a car. If personal accountability extended to every circumstance and experience, then this incident becomes your fault. You tell yourself that you should not have been walking down that sidewalk, at that particular time. Nothing productive comes from that. In fact, what is fostered is a delusion that somehow you are all knowing and have complete control over your circumstances.

There is a limit to *healthy* accountability. And although most people struggle with acknowledging a level of accountability that is natural and healthy, it can sometimes be taken too far.

Healthy accountability is never about assigning fault or blame. There are times when your actions clearly caused a particular situation – you were technically at "fault" for what happened. You can be at fault and deny it, or you can be at fault and own it. The difference is not the cause; the difference is the willing acceptance of the fault. The dominant societal definition of accountability is synonymous with blame, and fault. In fact, the word *accountability* is used in defining these terms. Words like *fault* and *blame* carry with them negative connotations and often lead to guilt – an emotion associated with remorse, sadness, and grief.

By contrast, accountability is not about guilt or grief, it is simply a recognition of the role you played in your situations, experiences, and outcomes. And when you extend accountability to include blame for everything that happens in your life, you are entering into the areas of guilt, sadness, and self-loathing.

With self-blame there is very little room for learning. You are simply not in a productive emotional state to learn. In fact, self-blame taken to an extreme can let you believe that there is no sense in trying to improve because there is something wrong with you that is outside your control to remedy. You can let yourself think that you are incapable of changing as a subconscious way to avoid the responsibility, and the work needed, to do better in the future.

Let's look at a hypothetical example. In an effort to clear your to-do list at work, you decide to squeeze in one more work call before leaving to pick up your daughter from school. Because that call ran longer than you had anticipated, you end up leaving later than you planned and getting caught in traffic, which delays you even further. When you finally get to your daughter's school, you are 30 minutes late. Immediately you blame yourself for your bad decision. You ask yourself, "What kind of parent would leave their kid standing there for half an hour?" You decide you must be the worst parent on the planet.

This takes accountability from recognizing your error, owning it, and learning from it, to wallowing in blame and self-pity: I'm a horrible parent! Playing the self-blame game is emotionally destructive. Self-blame is a cognitive process in which an individual attributes the occurrence of a stressful or unpleasant event to oneself. It tends to amplify our perceived inadequacies, which can lead to depression and a feeling of helplessness. There is a big difference between looking back at how my choices and behavior impacted the situation and others, versus blaming myself.

When you habitually blame yourself, your mental focus is on self-punishment, which only leads to being stuck and powerless to change. Self-blame inhibits the true power of accountability. The more accountable mindset lies simply in taking mental ownership of getting better.

Accountability isn't synonymous with blame. Healthy accountability instead embodies the concept of assumed innocence. Assumed innocence is the notion that you made the best possible choice in the moment, given what you knew at the time. This acknowledges that we have limited knowledge and understanding, and that we can fool ourselves by pretending not to know something when we want an outcome badly enough. Further, we can never fully know everything there is to know about a particular situation, especially the full extent of the consequences of each of the choices that are available to us at any moment in time. This is not an excuse for ineffective or even bad choices; it simply recognizes the limitations we face as part of the human condition, and this viewpoint gives us some grace when things don't turn out as planned.

When the same hypothetical situation is viewed through the lens of assumed innocence, there is no negative self-blame; and as a result you are much better positioned to objectively assess, learn, and adapt. Accountability is not about excusing a behavior or outcome, but it's also not about covering yourself in blame and guilt. Rather, accountability is about owning your actions and your outcomes. Essentially, accountability is a guilt-free zone.

With healthy accountability it's important to focus on what you can control. You cannot change the past, nor do you control the future. What you do control are your moment-by-moment actions. Just to be clear, blaming yourself is not taking ownership of your actions, and neither is feeling guilty over them. The positive impact that accountability can create is missed when it is viewed only as fault.

When you take ownership of a particularly bad situation or outcome and avoid the trap of self-blame, you are powerfully positioned to make an objective assessment of what actually happened and thereby enabled to identify the actions that ultimately created it. This is the true power of accountability – the recognition of how the actions that you chose contributed to the negative outcome, and your ability to choose more effectively in the future.

It's not that accountable people don't make mistakes – don't blow it – they do. It's just that accountable people learn from those situations and thereby are less likely to make the same or a similar mistake in the future. Each time this happens, the accountable person grows in wisdom and understanding, enabling them to be more successful in the future.

BEING ACCOUNTABLE IN AN UNACCOUNTABLE WORLD

We've discussed at length the benefits of being accountable, and in this chapter we have looked at the limitations of healthy accountability. Let's now turn our attention for a moment to what it means to be accountable in an unaccountable world.

As we discussed earlier, many people tend to live their lives more as victims than as "accountables." In fact, our language doesn't even have a name for accountable people like it does for those who are not accountable: *victims*. These labels themselves are not all that helpful in that all of us have a mix of accountable and unaccountable thinking patterns. Accountability is more of a spectrum than an on–off switch.

This implies that accountable people likely have victim thinking in some areas of their life, but if they are generally seeking to be more accountable, they will seek to identify those areas and work to take greater ownership. In this way, accountability is a life stance that fosters continual growth and engenders a willingness to shift away from victim-thinking patterns and behaviors. The following graphic illustrates the sweet spot on accountability, where you are accountable for what you can control – and *not* accountable for what you can't.

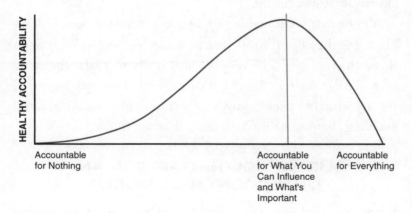

It would be a wonderful world if everyone in it were account-able for what they can control, but unfortunately, that is far from the case. I'm reluctant to say that the truly accountable person is *rare,* but I will say that at the very least, they are in the minority. That means that when you live your life accountably, you are by default uncommon and somewhat of a misfit. As an "uncommon misfit," there are some things that you need to be aware of.

Because society often promotes and embraces the victim mindset, one thing you are bound to experience as you take an accountable stance in life is that you become an easy target for others to blame for their mistakes. When others see you as someone who is willing to admit and own your mistakes, it's a mixed blessing. Some people will find that courageous and refreshing. Others won't understand it and will see you as a potential scapegoat for their problems and missteps. This risk can be particularly acute in the workplace.

Every group culture is different, and unfortunately, many cultures are full of finger pointing, blaming, and negative consequences. These social environments make it especially challenging to be accountable. When all those around you are avoiding accountability and shifting the blame, you, as a person who owns your mistakes, can easily become a target.

When I was a kid, we played "pile on" every chance we got. My dad would be laying on the floor in the living room watching TV and one of us would see him and yell out "Pile on!" then all three of us would jump on him. If I was outside with my friends and one of them fell to the ground for any reason, someone would inevitably shout, "Pile on!" and every kid within earshot was jumping on the pile. That game was fun for everyone except the unfortunate kid at the bottom of the pile!

It can feel like that in certain companies, where the "pile-on trolls" are constantly on the prowl for someone else to blame for their shortcomings. Don't be surprised or caught off guard when this happens. If you are part of a project that is behind schedule and will not meet the delivery date, it's important that you acknowledge your contribution to the delay, if in fact your actions contributed to it. But don't let other members of the team pile on by highlighting your action as the sole or primary cause of the late delivery, when there were other, critical mistakes made.

It's important that you stand on the truth. Be accountable for your actions, but don't take the blame for others. In this way, you may influence others to grow in accountability as well.

Another thing that can happen in an unaccountable world is that accountable people have a tendency to make others uncomfortable. Because the accountable person stands out from the crowd, their presence can be a reminder for others of their habit of avoiding responsibility. When one person is accountable, it creates a stark contrast with those who are not. You might be judged as intolerant or unsympathetic to the difficulties of those who have chosen victimhood. When this happens, you may find some people will try to exclude you, whether it's from joint projects at work or social gatherings with friends. I think it's important to remind yourself that they are not rejecting you as a person but are trying desperately to avoid facing their own lack of ownership.

6

ACCOUNTABILITY DOESN'T MEAN WHAT YOU THINK IT MEANS

Janet is a young lady with lots of talent. She is a middle manager with potential to rise in the organization. The problem is that Janet's boss, we'll call him Tom, has been trying to "hold" Janet accountable.

Tom is like most managers and leaders in that he has learned that to get his team to perform, he needs to hold them accountable. That is what his leadership preaches. That is how he is managed. In fact, that's all Tom's ever experienced. Perhaps you can relate. This is how most, practically all, companies practice accountability.

Most companies we've worked with, and Michael and I have worked with hundreds in just about every industry sector, take this approach to accountability.

Janet attended a workshop of ours, and when we began talking about accountability and how most leaders strive to hold their people accountable, Janet spoke up and shared her situation being on the receiving end of it. Listen to how Janet described her experience.

"I am so frustrated with my boss. Truthfully, I can't stand him. He's always trying to hold me accountable and creating negative consequences to try and force me to do what he thinks is best. It doesn't make me want to perform. In fact, it has the opposite effect. I don't want to even be in the same room with him. I give him the minimum effort just to keep him off my back. I'm capable of so much more. I've put in for a transfer. If that doesn't come through, I'll look for a new company."

Keep in mind, Janet is not some lacky; she is extremely bright and very capable. And her response is not extreme; it's actually quite common.

The problem for Tom and Janet is that this is what happens when a leader tries to hold his team accountable. It actually creates the exact opposite of accountability; it creates minimal performance with collateral damage. I'm fairly certain that the first time Tom interacted with Janet in this way it most likely didn't instantly create the disdain that Janet holds for Tom. But over time this is how it plays out.

Think about the last time someone tried to hold you accountable; what's your natural tendency? It's to resist, to push back, to defend yourself from what feels like an attack. And when the conversation ends, how are you left feeling? Do you feel like performing at your best? Are you inspired to go the extra mile? Are you committed to doing whatever it takes to accomplish your goals? Not hardly. More than likely, you're left feeling defeated, frustrated, angry, and resentful that you were treated that way. Meanwhile, the manager thinks he's done his job, he's held you accountable. This scene is then repeated over, and over, and over again.

I want to make sure you caught what Janet said. She said, "I give him the minimum effort." That is exactly what you get when you try and hold people accountable; you get the bare minimum.

We would argue that you can't "hold" someone accountable. We like to joke that you can hold a baby or a bag of groceries, but you can't hold someone accountable. When you peel that back, you uncover what it really means, which is to create a negative consequence when the person doesn't do what you want them to do. That is not accountability, that's management by consequences. Yes, consequences shape behavior, but you will never get discretionary effort with negative consequences. On the contrary, they produce just enough performance to stop the negative consequences, and, as we've pointed out, they come with collateral damage that ranges from passive resistance to outright sabotage.

The reason for the resistance is that the practice of holding someone accountable completely ignores the fact that the individual has choice. So, the individual instinctively fights back to stand their ground and prove that they do have personal choice. It is actually an unconscious, automatic response. You try to usurp my freedoms and I will naturally push back. It's important that you understand that employees are not intentionally being difficult or insubordinate. They are simply responding to your threat by standing their ground. One way or another, they will let you know that they have choice.

Trying to hold someone accountable is based on the flawed notion that you can force someone to do something. The truth is, you can't. You may create a consequence that is so distasteful, so unappealing that they choose to take a desired action, but that is where the damage happens.

Yet this is exactly how most companies operate. They manage through consequences and then wonder why the team isn't motivated and performing better. Consequence management is efficacious to a degree and that's why so many leaders apply it, but it's much like a parent–child model for toddlers and young children. When children are young, they don't possess the cognitive ability to reason and understand like adults do, so consequences are the primary method used to shape behavior. That may work for little kids, but it doesn't optimize the performance of adults. Yet, too often this parent–child model is mirrored in the boss–employee relationship.

You've likely seen this play out a thousand times. The employee is not performing to standard, not behaving as expected, and the boss steps in with a negative consequence to reshape the employee's behavior. One of the problems with negative consequences is that they tend to be relatively effective at stopping a specific behavior, but that doesn't guarantee that a productive behavior will replace it. In addition, to stop the unproductive behavior the manager, the arbiter of the consequences in this situation, needs to be ever present to deliver the consequences each and every time the behavior presents itself. This ultimately limits the number of employees the manager can supervise. And by the way, doesn't that sound like a fulfilling job: Keep a vigilant watch out for unproductive behavior, and then punish the perpetrator the minute you spot it?

As the manager administers the negative consequence, which can range from a stern scolding, to written reprimands, to threat of termination, the employee often fights back. The manager then doubles down by increasing the intensity of the consequences in an effort to establish authority. Whether this ends in the employee acquiescing or the manager firing her, either scenario is a bust.

Multiply this over the number of managers and employees in your company and think about the impact that is having on morale and the culture it is creating. Organizations that manage through consequences are getting less than optimal performance from their people and in many cases are getting the bare minimum. It's easy to spot a company that uses consequences to hold their people accountable. These companies have poor to mediocre performance, high turnover, and low morale.

Holding people accountable creates a culture of blame and excuse making; it creates a culture of low performance and an entitlement mindset.

A Better Way

Clearly, holding employees accountable is unproductive, not effective, and detrimental in so many ways. There is an alternative: Hold them *capable*.

Where holding accountable relies on consequences and threats, holding capable is essentially the opposite. The act of holding someone capable involves one individual, the leader in this context, confronting another individual, the employee, with their freedom and choices. This act recognizes that true accountability cannot be forced but rather occurs as an inevitable outgrowth of freedom.

It shifts the relationship from parent–child to a partnership. It redefines the role of leadership from treating employees as resources and managing, coercing, and manipulating behavior, to confronting employees with the freedom and responsibility to learn, develop, and perform. It shifts the burden of performance from the manager to the employee. The manager

is no longer responsible for the employee's behavior and performance – the employee is, which is naturally the case. The
manager then is free to be a coach, a mentor, and a guide providing opportunities for their direct reports to learn, adapt,
and grow.

Each individual is responsible for their choices and their
outcomes. The consequences of performance that occur come
about as a clear and organic result of the choices made, a
cause–effect relationship, not from a seemingly arbitrary
decision made by the manager.

This is not to say that the manager doesn't apply consequences when confronting with choice. There are times
when the manager is required to apply consequences. But the
employee understands that the actions taken by management
are in alignment with, and result from, the choices they made.
In the end we all choose our consequences by the choices we
make each and every day. Holding your people capable is not
passive; it's actually quite confrontive. But it is confrontive
with freedom and choice versus consequences. It is subtle but
profoundly different.

When an organization holds its people capable, everything
changes. The conversations change. The relationships change.
The results change. The culture changes.

With the acknowledgment of freedom comes true empowerment. Team members operate from a position of security
and confidence. They are more creative, more motivated, more
committed, more likely to seek input from others. When
confronted with their freedom of choice employees put forth
more effort, deliver higher quality of work, and consistently
perform at a higher level. And the ones who choose not
to perform are in essence choosing to leave, which is ultimately

a good outcome for both the employee and the company. Stop holding your people accountable; instead hold them capable.

Think about how you manage your top performers. You're not trying to hold them accountable, employing negative consequences to get them to perform. You might argue that you don't have to because they perform, and that's fine. But think about what you do with them. You connect them to the bigger vision. You challenge them to accomplish even more. You help them confront the breakdowns and encourage them to pursue new opportunities. You foster learning and development. You recognize and praise their progress and successes. No wonder they are doing well. You've partnered with them to enable them to achieve their best. You are holding them capable!

Why is it then that when someone is underperforming we take a completely different approach and try and force higher performance through negative consequences? Partly because that is what we've been taught. Partly because it seems more expedient in the moment. In addition, often the fundamental elements that are required to hold someone capable are not in place. We'll talk more about this in Chapter 9.

A Culture of Capability

The benefits of an accountable culture are clear to most leaders. In fact, when we train leaders and ask them to list the benefits of accountability, we always get the same answers: learning, growth, effective communication, trust, high performance, self-esteem, confidence, and better results.

Leaders have long known that accountability drives results. Accountable people are easier to lead, and accountable teams can accomplish great things. In fact, leaders are so aware of the importance of accountability that there's a huge industry that markets and sells "accountability systems" to companies seeking to enforce accountability.

"Accountability systems" are sought after because they measure individual performance. And while we believe that measurement is critical to establishing true accountability, the way that measurement systems are typically applied by leaders is more likely to lower accountability than to increase it. In essence, most systems that claim to be accountability systems create the opposite effect on your team.

This is because systems are not accountability. Systems are just tools. Accountability doesn't exist in systems, methods, or procedures. At the individual level accountability is a character trait, the foundation of high performance. Accountable people are people who have taken ownership of their responsibilities, goals, and dreams, as well as the actions needed to achieve them. Accountable teams exist only as collections of accountable individuals.

American leadership by and large has mistaken consequence-management systems for accountability systems, and the two systems are antithetical to one another.

A few years ago, John Doerr wrote the book *Measure What Matters*.[1] In the book he establishes the value of what he calls OKRs. OKR stands for objectives and key results. The premise of the book is that measuring what matters drives improved results.

Of course, we agree that measurement is necessary to improve performance. However, there is a point beyond which you cannot improve results if you're using measurement as part of a consequence-management system. The real potential

[1] John Doeer, *Measure What Matters: How Google, Bono, and the Gates Foundation Rock the World with OKRs*, 9780525536222 (April 24, 2018).

of your team can only be realized by using measurement as part of an ownership system that is designed to hold people capable.

A capable culture is one that embraces free-will choice and the freedom and anxiety that comes with it. A culture that fosters ownership at every level with clarity of expectation and a distinct connection between individual actions and collective results. The characteristics of a high-performance culture are built on a foundation of ownership. Characteristics such as trust, a bias for action, continuous learning, collaboration, innovation, communication – all of these are fostered and practiced more effectively when ownership is present. The challenge for leaders is to approach improvement opportunities in partnership with their employees.

You cannot create ownership through consequences. In fact, consequences impede innovation, collaboration, learning, trust, and most other traits that enable high performance. Take any one of these – let's use trust as an example. Holding others accountable creates blame, deflection, and excuses, among other things. Does that sound like an environment that is conducive to high trust? Quite the contrary. So, what do many executives do? They invest heavily in training programs in an effort to improve and enhance trust. Unfortunately, until you change how you view and engage with accountability, the training will likely have little lasting effect.

Another common program used to foster a high-performance culture is continuous learning. Creating a culture in which an organization embraces continuous learning can pay big dividends, with ongoing improvements occurring across the business. The creation of a learning culture requires that leaders encourage and allow trial and error. That is completely at odds with a "hold the team accountable" approach. When the leaders and the culture preach and apply a credo of continuous learning *and* of holding others accountable, now you have a serious conflict. The two are not symbiotic, and in fact are largely incompatible. By default, people will try to avoid the negative consequences that come with this view of accountability and not expose themselves by risking errors and failed attempts. As a result, the efforts to get the organization to embrace continuous learning are undermined and often produce very little in the way of lasting results.

It's the same with most (if not all) of the values that organizations pursue in an effort to be their best. Until you shift how the leaders, and the entire company, view and apply accountability, employees at all levels will struggle to truly live the promoted values.

When accountability is understood and embraced as free-will choice and ownership, now you have a powerful foundation to build and foster other desirable traits throughout the company. Let's go back to trust as an example: Trust and blame do not coexist very well together. Trust and ownership, though, are mutually reinforcing. The same is true with continuous learning, as well as innovation, collaboration, and the other high-performance traits that drive sustained success in the marketplace. When you get accountability right, other desirable values naturally follow.

As a leader, how you think about accountability affects virtually every aspect of your business and personal life.

This approach to accountability doesn't mean that everyone will perform well, only that they will perform to their capabilities. They may not have some key skill that is required for success, and they may be let go. They may not be a good fit, but that does not make them a bad person.

7

THE
CONSEQUENCES
METHOD

The prevailing method to drive results within most companies, as we have already mentioned, is the consequence model. Nearly every company that we have worked with over the years embraces some variation of this approach, whether they do so consciously or unconsciously. I'm not sure there has really ever been much of an alternative.

Despite the widespread use of consequence management systems, very few leaders have ever been formally trained in the *effective* use of consequences, and even fewer are aware of their inherent limitations.

The predominant behavioral science paradigm currently in use posits that there are four types of behavioral consequences: two that increase behavior and two that decrease it. The two that increase behavior are *positive* and *negative reinforcement*, and the two that decrease behavior are *punishment* and *penalty*.

Positive reinforcement is defined as a consequence that is perceived as desirable by the performer, and thereby increases the likelihood of a behavior being repeated. In other words, the individual gets something they want when they take a desired action. These consequences range from verbal praise and recognition to increased compensation and promotion.

Negative reinforcement is a consequence that is perceived as adverse by the performer and decreases the likelihood of a behavior being repeated. An example of this might be receiving a verbal reprimand from your boss because you didn't take a desired action. In this scenario, the performer will desire to avoid the negative consequence in the future by taking the appropriate action and thereby eliminating the need for the reprimand.

Punishment occurs when an individual gets something they don't want after they exhibit an undesirable behavior.

Penalty is the loss of something an individual desires when they exhibit an undesirable behavior.

Increase Behavior

Positive reinforcement – get something you want.

Negative reinforcement – avoid something you don't want.

Decrease Behavior

Punishment – get something you don't want.

Penalty – lose something you have that you want to keep.

Each type of consequence has a different effect on the behavior that it follows. It is important to note that, ultimately, consequences are experienced as either positive or negative based on the perspective of the performer receiving them. For example, public recognition for a job well done might be perceived by one individual as positive, and by another, who is made to feel uncomfortable by public recognition, as negative. This is just one source of the noise that is inherent in every consequence management system. Let's take a deeper look at each one of the four consequences, beginning with positive reinforcement.

POSITIVE REINFORCEMENT

Positive reinforcement is any consequence that follows a behavior and increases its frequency in the future. It occurs in one of two ways, natural and created. Natural reinforcements are outcomes that arise automatically after a behavior, while created reinforcement must be added by a person.

Examples of naturally occurring positive reinforcements include drinking coffee and becoming more alert, praising an acquaintance and improving the relationship, eating a meal and feeling satisfied, or conducting a no–cell phone time block and being more productive. These reinforcements occur naturally after a behavior triggers them.

Created reinforcements are applied directly by a person, or through a system. Examples of these types of consequences include thank-you notes, words of praise, positive public acknowledgments, meaningful trophies or plaques, or audio/visual "rewards" generated by an achievement in a video game. Created reinforcements can be either social or tangible. *Social* can involve saying or doing something positive for another person, while *tangible* is typically an item valued by the individual. The research indicates that the most effective positive reinforcement is social.

One of the challenges with positive reinforcement is that it is highly individualistic. What one person perceives as positive or pleasant, another may dislike. Some people appreciate public recognition, while others find it uncomfortable and embarrassing. One person may work extra hard for an additional $100, while another wouldn't get out of their chair for it.

In spite of this, the research has shown that positive reinforcement is the most effective consequence for encouraging desired behaviors and positive results.

As powerful as positive consequences are, in many companies their potential influence is diminished because the positive reinforcements are often delayed. Annual bonuses and clubs, monthly recognition, compensation increases, and promotions are all consequences that are not immediate – they are experienced in the future. Consequences are most effective when they follow immediately after a specific behavior. More about this later.

NEGATIVE REINFORCEMENT

Negative reinforcement, as I stated earlier, is an unpleasant consequence that occurs when an individual doesn't exhibit a specific desired behavior. The consequence that is delivered is intended to be unpleasant or undesirable by the person who is receiving it. For example, when you show up to a meeting late, your boss criticizes you in front of your peers. As long as it's not just the boss letting off steam, the hope is that the unpleasant criticism (negative consequence) will cause you to be on time for the next meeting.

If negative reinforcement and punishment seem similar to you, it's because they are. The difference is whether the consequence increases a productive behavior (negative reinforcement) or decreases an unproductive behavior (punishment).

In certain situations, negative reinforcement can be effective. We all learn not to touch a hot stove, either because Mom slapped our hand as we tried or we got burned. We learn to put gas in the car before the tank is completely empty in order to avoid the consequences of being stranded on the side of the road. There are, however, serious limitations and drawbacks with negative consequences, especially those that are applied by management. The first issue is that while negative reinforcement works fairly well in circumstances where all you need is compliance to a rule or regulation, or where you want a minimum level of performance, negative reinforcement will not produce discretionary effort beyond the minimum performance needed to avoid the consequence.

The second, and even more concerning drawback to negative reinforcement is similar to the drawbacks for punishment and penalty in that it creates collateral damage. Think about the example of getting reprimanded by your boss in front of your peers, and how that might make you feel resentful of your boss and the company. Every negative consequence, whether designed to increase behavior or decrease it, comes with collateral damage that ranges from resentment to outright sabotage.

Two of the most common consequences employed by management are punishment and penalty. Think back to the definition of accountability in Webster's online dictionary – all of the examples of accountability were negative in nature, and most were examples of punishment for poor performance.

PUNISHMENT

Punishment is a consequence that occurs after an undesirable behavior that is not wanted by the performer. As a child, you bit your sibling and you got a time-out. The intent of punishment is to create an experience that is so unpleasant that the performer will not repeat the behavior.

PENALTIES

Penalties are consequences that take away something the individual already has and wants. Your teenager comes home after the agreed-upon time and loses access to their phone or the family car for a week.

Both punishment and penalties can be effective at stopping unwanted behavior, but they do not cause a desired behavior to increase. Given that, punishment and penalty should be used primarily in situations where behavior is unsafe, illegal, or damaging.

HOW TO APPLY CONSEQUENCES

For any of these consequences to effectively shape behavior, there are three aspects that need to be considered. The first aspect is positive or negative. The second aspect is immediate or future. And the third aspect is certain or uncertain:

1. *Positive or negative.* This aspect looks at whether the consequence is positive or negative from the *performer's* perspective.
2. *Immediate or future.* This considers whether the consequence occurs as the behavior is happening (immediate), or sometime in the future.
3. *Certain or uncertain.* If the consequence occurs every time the behavior happens, then it is certain; anything less creates uncertainty.

All four types of consequences (positive, negative, punishment, penalty) are subject to impact erosion, meaning that they are most effective when they occur immediately and with certainty. That is what makes actions like dieting and saving (money) so difficult. Both dieting to lose weight and saving to increase wealth are situations where the immediate consequences (eating less or being frugal) are negative and certain, and the positive consequences (better health or financial security) are future and uncertain. This gap between the timing and certainty of consequences is the common scenario played out in most companies – the positive consequences like bonuses, raises, and promotions are most often future and uncertain, and the negative consequences (like verbal reprimands, written warnings, and loss of privileges) are predominately immediate and certain.

As an example, let's look at a salesperson and the productive behavior of making calls to new prospects. The benefits to making the calls are obvious. When the rep makes calls, she sells more of the company's products or services. Selling more leads to increased recognition and more money – both very desirable consequences for most salespeople. Unfortunately, increased recognition and higher income are both future and uncertain. In many situations, the sales process isn't completed on the first call, so even if the rep is successful with the initial call, it doesn't necessarily translate into a sale.

Let's contrast that with the natural consequences a salesperson experiences immediately when making a sales call – discomfort, potential rejection, and doubt. Not only are these consequences immediate, but in most cases they are certain or nearly so. These consequences are the reason that salespeople are often told by their managers, "Don't worry about the rejection, it's just a numbers game."

The natural consequences for *not* calling are virtually the opposite. By avoiding the calls, the rep not only avoids the negative consequences of discomfort and rejection but also creates more time for activities that she enjoys. Looking at it from this perspective, it's a wonder that any sales reps ever make outbound calls to prospects. The natural consequences that arise from calling actually inhibit sales calls.

If we stay with this example, it gets even more interesting. Typically, at this point the manager steps in with some form of negative consequence, a punishment or penalty. It may be a chewing out or the threat of losing a perk. If we analyze this consequence, we can see that it clearly is negative, but what about the immediacy and the certainty? It might be immediate on one or two occasions, but for it to be immediate and certain every time, the manager would need to be hovering over the sales rep continually. That is not likely to happen.

Most often, the designed or systemic consequences for not calling are experienced days later when they attend the weekly sales meeting with their boss. Further, as we pointed out earlier, the negative consequences arising in the sales meeting will likely damage the leader/employee relationship, potentially making the employee even less likely to exhibit the desired behavior consistently.

Unfortunately, the consequences in many organizations are misaligned in this way, and too often are also primarily negative. Negative consequences in general can be useful in stopping a particular behavior, as stated earlier. If someone is doing something that is unsafe or unethical, a negative consequence can stop the person from continuing with the action. The usefulness for curbing the action long-term is uncertain, though. For the consequence to have a lasting effect, often you will need to apply it multiple times. That means you will need to catch the person in the act more than once and apply the consequence each time for it to have any real lasting impact. Over time, if the behavior persists, the manager is forced to increase the "volume" of the consequence. You can in some instances create such a severe negative consequence that the individual on the receiving end is so frightened or traumatized that the action is never again repeated. However, this comes at a high relationship cost.

Stopping undesirable behavior with negative consequences has enough challenges, but to make matters worse, too often negative consequences are also used in an effort to produce a productive behavior.

Applying a negative consequence may successfully stop an unwanted behavior, but there is no guarantee it will be replaced with a productive one. Most companies, most managers, misuse negative consequences in an effort to drive positive performance. This is the primary concept that underlies "holding your team accountable."

If someone is not performing, a manager is often taught to *get after them*. This almost always means some form of negative consequence. That would be fine if you could consistently produce a positive action with a negative consequence, but it doesn't work that way. You are using a negative consequence best used to stop a behavior to add pressure for a desired behavior. Often, this approach creates the opposite effect, in that it damages the relationship and creates animosity toward the manager and the company.

Consequences are also misapplied in many situations. It's possible that the employee isn't even clear what the desired behavior is, may not be skilled in performing it, or both. Misapplied consequences will only make matters worse.

Negative consequences are intended to be offset by the positive consequences established as part of the overall consequence system – a beautiful yin–yang balance. As we pointed out, the company makes it painful when employees don't perform and pleasurable when they do. The assumption is that in this delicate balance of consequences, the employee will gravitate toward the rewards. The problem is that the rewards are usually associated with the results and are only experienced at a point in the future, while the pain is typically associated with the behavior and experienced in the present. This necessitates that each employee have a long-term orientation with respect to their current situation. Unfortunately, that is not the case for most people. The promise of a potential and distant reward is greatly overshadowed by the unpleasantness of taking an unlikable action in the moment. We all are wired for comfort and act to optimize the current situation. That is why a negative consequence works to stop a behavior, but using it to entice a productive one only creates frustration and bitterness for the one on the receiving end.

The employee receiving the punishment comes to resent the company and the manager. In fact, the employee often views the punishment as a mean-spirited discretionary act (and with certain managers, it may be). In fact, punishment subtly implies that the performer intended to fall short or to fail. Punishment for people who intended to perform well but failed – due to lack of training, opportunity, vagaries of the workplace, or even a lack of awareness that they were expected to perform a task at all – is usually counterproductive at best, and relationship damaging at worst.

Further, an employee often fails to associate the consequence with a specific behavior altogether and simply blames the manager for picking on them. The experience for the employee in many cases has very little to do with their behavior or performance and everything to do with how much of a jerk the manager is. Rarely does a negative consequence cause employees to reflect on their performance – instead, they often instinctively lash out. But because the manager holds the power to terminate their employment, they have to find subtle ways to get back at the manager (nothing too overt, or they may lose their job).

Just to be clear, we are not saying that consequences are "bad." Consequences help shape behavior. As a leader, you need solid performance standards to be upheld, and you will need to apply consequences, both positive and negative. But consequences are not, and never will be, *accountability*.

8

CAPABLE
LEADERSHIP

Personal accountability is rooted in the fundamental human ability to choose. Productive choices lead to higher performance, facilitate learning and growth, and increase fulfillment. A corporate focus on fostering individual choice puts decision power where it belongs – in the hands of the person charged with doing the work – and as an additional and highly valuable benefit it reduces the workload for leaders.

In a consequence management system on the other hand, performers are encouraged to optimize a suite of consequences that have been created and/or amplified by management. The performer's focus in these systems is not necessarily on optimizing overall outcomes, but rather on managing and manipulating the consequences of the system. In other words, employees will optimize *their* consequence outcomes, not necessarily the overall system outcomes.

When a performer is in a system where consequences are the primary lever to drive performance, workers rarely achieve what they are truly capable of. With consequence management, you can produce improved results in certain situations, but not what your team is ultimately capable of, and you will likely experience pushback on the process and resentment against you as the leader.

Consequence management is based on someone with organizational power (the leader) coercing someone with less organizational power (their direct reports) to take specific actions deemed to be desirable by the leader. When a performer sees the manager as the broker of consequences, they often feel marginalized and manipulated and they resist the system.

The traditional and widespread management by consequence model often creates the opposite of what management intends. Instead of greater levels of accountability, consequence management creates greater levels of entitlement. To get at the missed potential of a performer, a leader must shift the focus from "holding them accountable" through consequences, to "holding them capable." That is, holding them capable of making productive choices for themselves and the systems that they operate within.

In the previous chapter, we discussed how management by consequences *can* often quickly improve results, but it *cannot* sustain positive performance gains without continuous reinforcement. Research shows that negative consequences *can* get people to perform up to minimum standards, or even occasionally achieve stretch goals, but they *cannot* get people to perform above the minimum effort required to avoid the negative consequences. Not only do consequences not optimize results, in fact they often have lasting downsides. The resentment deriving from a consequence management system creates a mindset of doing the minimum necessary to avoid the negative consequences.

Interestingly, a Gallup study conducted in 2015 found that more than half of all employees did the minimum required at work and would leave quickly for a marginally better opportunity.

Since the manager and the performer in a consequence management system focus on optimizing the consequence model, not on optimizing ultimate outcomes, the gap between the two approaches (consequences vs. ownership) cannot be bridged. To tap into what you and your team are capable of, it is necessary to shift from the consequence model to focusing instead on ownership.

Consequence management is something that a manager "does" to others, whereas fostering an ownership mindset in others requires the participation of both parties toward a common goal (the success of the performer and the system). In this chapter, we argue that working to build an ownership mindset, and a team culture of ownership, is the highest purpose of leadership.

To facilitate the performance and growth of individuals and teams most effectively, the consequence-first model must be abandoned. Stop trying to "hold people accountable," and instead "hold them capable." Challenge them to take ownership of their own capabilities, choices, and successes.

When a leader shifts to helping a team member embrace their capabilities, the employee is acknowledged as an equal partner with their manager – which is the underlying reality of the relationship, regardless of the performance model being used. The manager no longer relies on the position power as manager to force an employee to hit standards, but instead helps an employee to choose what the employee feels is personally best. These changes are long lasting, because once employees grasp their own power to choose success or to seek other opportunities more aligned with their personal objectives, there is no going back to the outdated command-and-control model of the past.

In this way, leaders can lead larger teams because they no longer have to *manage the minutia*. Instead, they become guides to those who want to grow, and help those who don't want to grow in their current role to leave and find a better fit for themselves elsewhere. Employees who embrace their own capabilities to perform and grow will seek out their manager when they encounter barriers and breakdowns. They will have greater courage (and permission) to make mistakes and to take risks, which facilitates continuous learning and improvement. The manager stops pushing, and shifts to enabling, which in the end requires a lot less time and effort.

CONSEQUENCES EXIST IN EVERY SYSTEM

Often when we train leaders, we get an interesting response. On the one hand, most are intuitively drawn to the notion of accountability as ownership. On the other hand, they often struggle with the application of the concept. We get questions like, "Are you saying we can't have or enforce high standards?" or "Don't we have the right to expect solid performance since we pay them to work?" These questions express an underlying fear that when we abandon the role as the consequence dealer, we lose all meaningful influence on performance. That somehow accountability as ownership is passive from the leader's perspective.

Let us be as clear as we can regarding consequences: We are not advocating the removal of consequences from performance systems. Consequences, in and of themselves, are essential to help shape behavior and learning, and they are inevitable in any system. Consequences are highly valuable in the process of making productive choices.

What we are saying is that consequences and accountability are not the same, and when leaders see themselves as the dealer of consequences, they are choosing an approach that undermines innovation and limits performance.

There are significant inefficiencies that arise when managers (often unconsciously) place themselves between a performer and the consequences of their performance.

As we've dicussed, significant relationship costs arise when leaders manage with consequences. Employees naturally see the leaders as choosing to deliver, or not to deliver, the negative and/or positive consequences they experience. Further, the leaders actually do set themselves up to show favoritism (also often unconsciously), based on their subjective thinking and feelings about specific individuals.

Managers who primarily use consequences to shape the behaviors of their teams can only partially tap into what the individuals on their teams are truly capable of. The effects of the negative consequences applied by managers linger much longer than the effects of the positive consequences, which generates minimal performance, and they can even lead to an entitlement mentality: "I did what you told me to do, and it didn't work. I want the positive outcomes you promised because I did what you said!"

Consequences are part of life and certainly part of business. As a leader, you will need to apply consequences, both positive and negative. The key is to not lead with consequences, but rather to confront with choice and highlight the connection between the performer's choices and the consequences experienced. Part of the role of the leader is to help each team member recognize the natural relationship between one's choices and the outcomes (consequences) they experience. This approach helps the performer to focus on what they can control and to personally confront their own motives and desires. The notion is straightforward: The consequences and outcomes one experiences in life are a byproduct of the choices they make and the actions they take. If you choose productive actions, you experience positive outcomes. If you choose unproductive actions, you experience less-than-desirable outcomes. The choice is always yours.

Again, let us be clear. Consequences are an important component for changing behavior and results. However, a consequence management system inherently creates suboptimal results and some significant issues in terms of engagement and mindset. There is a better way to help people accomplish what they are capable of.

THE POWER OF HIGH EXPECTATIONS AND STANDARDS

Sometimes, when leaders hear us say, "Don't manage with consequences," and that accountability is free-will choice, some managers think they hear us saying, "Have low expectations and tolerate low performance." They also hear that what we propose to do instead is very passive (let people do what they want). That is the opposite of what we are saying. In fact, there is statistical evidence[1] that high standards are part of any effective performance model, especially one that seeks to hold people capable rather than accountable. The mechanics of the two approaches look similar – the differences are subtle. But the difference in team and individual performance is significant and markedly better.

---

[1] David H. Maister, *Practice What You Preach,* The Free Press, ISBN 0-7432-1187-1.

In 2001, David H. Maister published the book *Practice What You Preach*. The book reviews the author's findings from a worldwide survey of "139 offices, in 29 firms, in 15 countries, in 15 different lines of business." What he and his researchers found was that "attitudes drive financial results, and not (predominantly) the other way round." Specifically, the study found that Quality & Client Relationships (QCR) was the most statistically significant factor in determining financial performance (a measure that averaged four equally weighted factors:

1. Two-year percentage growth in revenues
2. Two-year percentage growth in profit
3. Profit margin
4. Profit per employee).

The study also found that QCR in turn was driven by a combination of high standards and employee satisfaction. Interestingly, employee satisfaction was driven by empowerment, coaching, and high standards. The headline from the Maister study is that high standards are absolutely a required component of organizational success and are an integral part of the process of holding people capable. Further, high standards actually *lead to higher* employee satisfaction.

The reality is that holding high standards alone will dramatically improve operating results. Four characteristics make high standards effective:

1. They align with the primary focus of the business.
2. They are challenging to achieve.
3. They are clearly defined.
4. They are consistently applied to everyone.

Ultimately, they become part of the culture and are reinforced and enforced by the team. You accept the standards, or you're not a good fit. The presence of high standards solves myriad issues and creates significant benefits, including:

- High standards improve employee satisfaction.
- Customer satisfaction goes up.
- Profitability goes up.
- Teamwork and cohesiveness increase.
- Performance expectations are clear and understood.
- Training and development are aligned to achieving the standards.
- Top-performing peers are admired and set a standard for the rest.
- Top performers are not resented by low performers – it's the other way around.
- They engage and motivate top performers.
- The best employees are consistently recognized and retained.
- Low performers are outplaced quickly.
- Drive a high-performance culture that is self-reinforcing – the entire team, not just the leader, confronts low performers and low performance.
- It's not pleasing the boss, it's hitting the standard.
- Favoritism is dampened – everyone is treated fairly (but not the same).

High standards define the desired performance of a group and the individuals that make up the group. Standards are an integral part of a culture. Individuals reinforce the standards themselves, and they don't tolerate poor performance from their peers. Where high standards are built into a culture, members who don't fit it won't make it. Standards communicate what is expected, what is nonnegotiable. Without high standards, a group will perform well below what they are capable of.

Accountability as ownership promotes a system of high standards that are nonnegotiable, and where team members own the standards. That system is not soft and undemanding; it is challenging and rewarding, and it calls on the individual to deliver their best.

TAKING OWNERSHIP OF THE STANDARDS

In our book *The 12 Week Year*, we define ownership as a character trait. It is a willingness to own one's actions and results regardless of the external circumstances. The very nature of ownership rests on the realization that everyone has freedom of choice regardless of the circumstances, and it is this freedom that underlies our view of accountability as ownership.

As a leader, you are free to set standards for performance. Employees in turn are free to accept those standards or to not accept them. If they choose not to, they are simply choosing not to work in your organization. They are not "bad" people; they are just not a good fit for the opportunity you are offering.

When an employee decides to take ownership of a set of standards, they are simultaneously taking ownership of the consequences associated with those standards. If they meet the standards, certain consequences will follow; if they fail to hit the standard, other consequences will follow. The manager has no say in the ongoing process of performance and consequences

beyond setting the initial standards and the resulting consequences.

Where the manager does get involved in the process is as a
mentor or coach. Coming alongside the employee and encouraging them to choose the consequences they desire by taking
the actions necessary to hit the standards. The choice to own,
or not own, the standards is the employee's alone.

THE ACCOUNTABLE MINDSET

The approach of holding people capable is not about lower-
ing your desire to achieve great things as a leader; it's about
helping your team members to connect with their desire to
accomplish great things for themselves and the organization.
The process of holding someone capable therefore begins when
a performer takes ownership of the standards and outcomes
expected in their role because those things represent greatness in
their role and they see how those accomplishments help them
achieve their most important personal objectives, aspirations,
and needs – the proverbial "what's in it for them." This is the
"Why" that underlies a performer's decision to join the company and to accept their position in it in the first place.

The elements of an accountable employee mindset are innumerable, but there are a few beliefs that are common in our
experience to all accountable people:

- My ego and fear are subsumed by my desire to excel.
- Poor results are not to be hidden from others to avoid punishment, but are signposts to areas where I can improve.
- Mistakes are learning opportunities, not intentional
  outcomes to be punished for.

- I am responsible for my own successes and failures. They're not someone else's doing; they are my outcomes arising from the choices I make.
- I have made intentional and clear connections between how success in my role helps me move toward my needs, goals, and aspirations in life.
- I see my manager and peers as partners in my growth and in my achievements, not as competitors or adversaries.
- I seek feedback and act on it rather than become defensive and avoid it.
- I have control over how I choose to think and act in every situation.
- I am the author of my own success in life.

As a leader, your role in the process of facilitating an ownership mindset and culture is to come up alongside the performers and explore, through joint discussion, what's truly important to them and to establish your role in helping them achieve those things.

This process is one of mentor-coach rather than cop-judge. To effectively lead through holding people capable, you must see your role as developing high performers, not as a consequence manager.

The leader's purpose is to help their team members accomplish what's important to *them*. To put their success as the leader's top priority. This means that the process starts with the leader's genuine interest in what's important to each team member in their lives. What are their aspirations, values, interests, skills, and capabilities? The leader's role is to first become a partner with them in accomplishing their aspirations, and then helping them as a coach to see how they control the outcomes they experience through their own choices. Ultimately, the leader's mindset is to help each team member realize that they control their destiny at work and in life through the choices they make each day and help them to continually make the productive choices that are aligned with what they want. As a leader, when you embrace accountability as choice, as ownership, it changes your actions, which in turn changes the conversations, the interactions, the relationships, the culture, and the results for you and your teams.

In Chapter 11, Putting It All Together, we provide some guidance for both individuals and leaders who want to optimize their results by effectively holding themselves and/or their teams capable.

9

HOLDING THE TEAM CAPABLE

As a leader, when you shift from accountability as consequences to accountability as personal ownership, it changes the way you lead and manage. As we have already pointed out, when your thinking shifts, your actions shift as well. Let's look at how this works in greater detail.

If my thinking (conscious or unconscious) is that I can hold someone else accountable, then the actions that naturally flow from that thinking center around trying to force my employees to take specific actions under the threat of punishment. The punishment can range from verbal chastisement, to the removal of favorable conditions, to increased oversight, to loss of perks, and ultimately firing. In fact, managers get pretty creative in finding new ways to "force" productive behaviors. In one company we worked with, if the sales reps didn't hit a minimum level of production, they were required to wash their manager's car and perform other humiliating tasks. (If at this point in the book you think you've just found a new technique to apply with your team, then stop reading and give the book to someone else – there is little hope for you!)

Contrast that with the thinking that accountability is ownership based on free-will choice. If that is my mindset as a leader, then a completely different set of actions arise. With the realization that I can't really force someone to do something (they always have choice), I'm challenged to find a different way to influence that fosters a personal choice on the part of my team members to take productive action. The first thing that changes when a leader's thinking shifts from consequences to ownership is the conversations they have with their team.

The conversation becomes two-way rather than one-way in which I tell my employee how it's going to be. Instead, I'm forced to engage my employee in a conversation around their actions and performance and what they want to achieve.

When I do this, two things happen. The first thing is that team members are now actively involved and participating in determining how they will overcome obstacles and barriers and produce better results. This is huge. This thinking shift cannot be overstated in terms of its impact. Each associate now actively participates in their own success and growth, a key step in creating ownership. The second thing is because it's a two-way conversation seeking truth, I learn more about the specifics – the obstacles, the barriers, the struggles – and more about my team member – their mindset, their level of competence, their level of confidence. I may even learn things that will change my approach to helping my team. My team in turn learns more about me, my thinking, and my motivation. In this way, the team begins to realize that as a leader I am less concerned about my own self-interests, and more concerned about my team members' success.

Because I no longer see punishment as the tool to lead with, I learn to confront with personal choice, rather than consequences. Confronting with choice is so much easier than confronting with consequences. Where negative consequences and the threat of punishment create tension and resentment and damage the relationship, confronting with choice has the opposite effect. It engages the employee emotionally and intellectually. It challenges and encourages them. It actually builds relationships.

The two-way conversation begins with a discussion on what constitutes acceptable performance. As a leader, it's critical that you don't lower the standard; instead, you work to raise the level of performance.

For a performer to be willing to change and to put the effort in to improve, they must first agree that their current level of performance is unsatisfactory. Without acknowledgment of the performance gap, there is no motivation for them to change. Too often, managers assume the performer knows and agrees that their performance is unacceptable, and the manager moves immediately to "fixing" the problem. That approach limits the opportunity for growth and creates relationship damage. Without joint agreement that a problem exists, any conversation about a fix is wasted time. The employee may listen, primarily because they feel they "have to," but little or nothing will change.

Standards are the first place where a leader has the opportunity to confront with choice. Just because there are standards doesn't alter the fact that the team member has choice. You will want to point out that they don't "have to" perform to standard, they only need that level of performance if they wish to continue to be a part of your team. They can always choose to work somewhere else. Not a bad person, just a bad fit for the role.

On the surface, this may seem no different than confronting with a threat – "You either step up or you're fired." The difference is – and this is a major difference – that they are in control, they decide which set of consequences they want to experience.

The employee is now faced with an important decision. Are they willing to do what it takes to maintain a level of performance to continue with you and your company, or do they want to work somewhere else? When you confront head-on with consequences, the performer is never asked to consciously choose. Do they really want to work here? Do they want to be successful here? Any other scenario is based on an unverified assumption of desire. In this approach, nothing is assumed; employees are asked to choose. When confronted in this way, the choice the employee makes will be the internal motivation for them to behave differently, one way or the other. There is less animosity and guilt when a leader confronts with choice.

Whether they choose to stay and perform or to leave, you can support them in their choice. Assuming they choose to stay and perform, you now have set the stage for them to fully engage in the effort to improve their performance. This is big. You are no longer "doing it to them;" you are now "doing it with them." This is what ownership looks like. The burden to perform is theirs, not yours, and both of you are clear about that. If they decide to leave, it can happen without all the typical drama and animosity, and with greater levels of mutual respect.

Let me share with you a real-world example. Michael and I had conducted a session on *Accountability as Ownership* with a group of front-line managers in an insurance company. Each of the participating managers had approximately 30–50 agents that they were responsible for within their territory. All of them had a group of agents that were identified as high performers. Unfortunately, this represented only a small fraction of their team. The bulk of the agents ranged between poor to solid performers, which meant that each manager had a number of agents who were underperforming and a tremendous opportunity for improvement with the majority of their agents.

"Phil," one of the managers who attended, left the workshop thinking about a particular agent of his that had started out strong, but over the past 12–18 months had struggled. In an effort to get the agent back on track, Phil had been using the traditional approach of "holding" the agent accountable and creating negative consequences for the individual. What frustrated Phil was that it was not having the effect he was hoping it would. In fact, the agent's results were actually getting worse and he was, in Phil's words, "checking out." So Phil figured he had little to lose by trying the different approach that he had just received training on.

Phil set up a meeting with the agent. He opened the conversation with a brief discussion about how he had been trying to hold the agent accountable and that he was no longer willing to do that. Phil pointed out that it was the agent's responsibility to perform, and that no matter how much Phil wanted him to be successful the agent had to be committed to his own success and be willing to do the work. Phil discussed why he hired the agent in the first place – the strengths, experience, and attitude that the agent possessed. They discussed what acceptable performance looked like and agreed that the agent's current level was not acceptable. They also talked about the behaviors and activity levels that are required to be a successful agent.

Then Phil confronted the agent with the choice: "Do you want to work here; do you want to be successful in this company; are you willing to do what it takes?"

The agent was somewhat surprised by the question. He had never really confronted it. He had been too consumed with a victim mindset, feeling like Phil was unfairly punishing him. He asked Phil for a few days to think about it. They reconvened a couple days later and what unfolded surprised Phil. This time the agent led the conversation. He thanked Phil for his candor and for his support. He then went on to apologize for his poor performance and attitude. He mentioned that he never intended to be "one of those people" who makes excuses and blames others for their lack of success. That is not who he is, or how he wants to be perceived. He told Phil he did want to be a successful agent, working with Phil, and that he was willing to do the things necessary to make it happen.

Phil was shocked – pleasantly so, but shocked. He fully expected the agent to quit, but was genuinely happy to hear the news. They went on to discuss the agent's goals and his tactical plan. Literally, that week the agent's attitude and behavior changed. Within a few weeks, it started to show in his results. And within a few months, he became one of Phil's better-performing agents.

Of course, not every situation concludes with an ideal ending like this one. It could have just as easily gone the other way, with the agent deciding to quit. Or it might have been a scenario where the agent stays but continues to struggle. Holding an employee capable doesn't guarantee that they will succeed, it just guarantees the best odds of success. When you have ownership on the part of the employee, you have the best chance of success.

Let's go back to the Results/Action/Thinking framework. When you *think* that you can hold someone accountable, then at the *action* level, you tend to lead with consequences: negative reinforcement, or more likely, punishment, when the associate is underperforming. The *results* are entitlement, resentment, and mediocre performance. The actions you take as a leader and the resulting mediocre performance are a natural byproduct of your thinking.

This framework is mirrored on a larger scale across the entire company. The collective beliefs of an organization drive specific behaviors that create predictable results. This makes sense, given that a company is simply a collection of individuals.

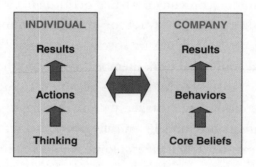

How you, and your organization, think about accountability affects practically everything that you do as an organization. As long as team members view accountability as consequences (whether consciously or unconsciously), the organization will continue to manage and manipulate through negative consequences and thereby limit the overall growth and success of the enterprise.

When the thinking shifts to the realization that accountability is ownership based on free-will choice, then a different set of behaviors emerge and the collective potential of the team is liberated, producing your best results.

Holding the team capable creates the most productive platform to unleash the highest levels of performance available from your people. The transition from a consequence-based approach to a choice-based one doesn't come without some challenges. One such challenge is that not everyone will embrace it.

As Peter Koestenbaum and Peter Block point out in their book *Freedom and Accountability at Work,* to hold the team capable requires that we confront our own need for control and our lack of faith in the people around us. Part of the reason the common consequence-based performance model exists is to provide a sense of control for management and a way to potentially predict and ensure specific outcomes. For a leader to recognize individual team member choice and then to operate from that place, the leader must be willing to surrender the perceived control they mistakenly think they have.

The consequence model ironically provides a safe haven for low performance. When an employee is told what to do, how to do it, and when it needs to be completed, they are effectively absolved from any failure that happens. After all, they were just doing what the boss told them to do. As unpleasant as the consequences may be, the employee will usually deflect and shift blame because they had no say in the way the project or task was designed; they were simply "following orders."

When a leader initially embraces the capable model, it can make some employees extremely uncomfortable with the exposure and responsibility that comes with it. The capable model requires employees to confront their own internal desires and choices, and removes the inherent excuses for poor performance. The burden to perform is clearly and squarely on their shoulders, and so is the freedom necessary to make it happen. Some, like Phil's agent in the story above, will embrace it, others will fight it, and some will choose to leave. All of those outcomes are good ones.

CRITICAL STRUCTURES

As a leader, if you are going to hold your people capable, there are some critical structures that will be necessary – the first of which is clarity of expectation, starting with vision. Not corporate vision, but rather your team members' personal vision. If you are going to confront them with their choices, then the performers, and you, need to know what they want in life.

This work on "why" is rarely done before the consequence model is invoked. Most managers shy away from "getting personal" with their employees. But as Michael and I have worked with clients and have helped them to engage with their team members around their individual personal visions, the results are often unexpected. What the manager experiences is not the resistance or awkwardness that they feared, but rather rich and meaningful conversations with their employees. And the employees leave inspired and feeling good about the company and the leadership. Remember, though, it's their vision, not yours. You can encourage, guide, and ask probing questions to help them build their vision, but the vision must remain theirs.

This is critical if you are going to help your employees connect the dots between succeeding in their role and living the life they want to live. That connection between their actions and their desires is the basis of all high performance. When a performer is clear on *their* near-term and long-term desires (vision), they are then empowered and compelled to make productive choices. Their vision becomes a powerful thread that connects their personal aspirations through the company vision and goals to their daily actions. This connection puts their actions in perspective, and creates both positive and negative consequences that naturally arise based on their choices. As each choice either moves them closer to their vision (positive) or away from it (negative) they choose their own results and consequences. This work on vision also builds intimacy, trust, and earns the leader the permission to coach and confront the employee with much less resistance.

An additional aspect of clarity needed to hold others capable is a tactical plan. In order to foster accountable performers, clear expectations are required – at the vision level, at the goal level, and most importantly at the action level. Only a fool would sign up to be accountable for something that is vague and unstructured. And yet that's what most companies ask of their employees, because most plans are conceptual, not tactical. With conceptual or directional plans, each individual is left on their own to determine what actions are most appropriate and productive. I'm all for giving people freedom, but this is setting them up to fail. If they guess right, everything is fine; if they guess wrong, the negative consequences will come raining down.

In some cases, a role may not be amenable to working from a traditional plan. Some people are in roles where they don't control their work triggers. Maybe their work begins when the phone rings, they get an order, or maybe they get an email that starts things off. They generally can't create a plan to answer the phone a certain number of times because they don't control their work triggers. In cases like these, clear performance expectations are still essential. Focus the expectations, not just on outcomes, but also on specific behaviors.

This lack of plan specificity is exacerbated by the annual planning process. Annual goal setting and planning are better than no planning at all, but they come with serious pitfalls and limitations. In March 2020, Covid hit the world. As companies and individuals were planning for the new year in late 2019 and early 2020, no one planned for a global pandemic. Very quickly the world experienced how ineffective annual planning is. Trying to plan tactically for 12 months is not practical or productive even in "normal" times. That is why most annual plans are conceptual. It's virtually impossible to know what actions people should be taking six months or more into the future.

We strongly recommend that you ditch your annual plan in favor of 12-week planning. Twelve months is not only difficult to plan for, but it also inherently encourages procrastination by creating the illusion that there is plenty of time to take action and accomplish goals. After all, you have a full year to make it happen, anything could happen! Ultimately, the annual cycle produces a lack of urgency, procrastination, and mediocre performance. A 12-week plan allows you to get granular and tactical. For more on 12-week plans, see our previous work titled *The 12 Week Year*.

Well-written tactical plans spell out the specific, discrete actions and timings that are needed to accomplish the goal.

A solid tactic describes an action that the performer can take when it comes due. All the vagueness and wiggle room of annual plans are removed. With a tactical plan there is absolute clarity regarding what actions are required. Enabling performers to have input into plan construction creates buy-in, and once established, there is no question about what is to be done. If you don't have a tactical plan, you will struggle to foster accountable performers.

The second structure that is required to hold people capable is execution transparency. Transparency in this context means operating in such a way that everyone can see what actions are being performed, and what actions are not. For individuals and teams to be accountable, you as the leader must eliminate the hiding places by removing the ambiguity that lets people avoid seeing and confronting the truth. You will need to ensure that the completion or lack of completion for each action in the plan is visible for all.

This transparency process involves two elements. The first is a method to measure, or score, individual and team execution consistently. When we created the 12 Week Year (for more information on this system visit 12weekyear.com), we introduced the concept of scoring or measuring your execution. Like most systems, we have you track your lead and lag indicators, but in addition, we have you score your weekly execution. This measure is the most powerful lead indicator you have, and is the greatest predictor of your probability of success. It creates absolute transparency by individual for every member of the team.

This is the most effective way we have found to assess weekly performance to the plan. The second element of transparency is a weekly forum where the team members review the week's planned actions and openly discuss what got done and what didn't. We call this a *weekly accountability meeting*, or a WAM. These two elements taken together create total transparency where performance is discussed and needed improvements are identified.

Whether you apply the 12 Week Year or not, you will need a process that ensures that the entire team has a view into what actions were completed each week, and has an opportunity to discuss the implications.

The final structure is evidence. At this point, each member of the team has a clear, compelling personal vision that connects to the company vision. They have clarity of what is expected of them – the actions they are to perform each week over the next 12 weeks. Now we need to know if the actions are creating the outcomes we thought they would. This requires measuring and tracking the results created by the execution of the plan.

Measurement in a "hold capable" system is information that helps performers get better. And they desire measurement because it helps them to improve; it's not a hammer to get hit with. In a "hold accountable" system, measurement is seen as the trigger for negative consequences.

Earlier we discussed the importance of knowing that we control our actions, not our outcomes. This is why you (and your team) will "score" your execution, your actions, and you will measure the results of your execution.

These four structures (vision, plan, transparency, and evidence) taken together create a system that fosters individual and team accountability and ownership. Without these structures in place, team members will be reluctant to own their actions or results, and you as the leader will lack the necessary elements to effectively confront and develop your employees. Without these critical structures, you will have no choice but to manage through consequences.

For more on these critical structures, we recommend our *New York Times* best-selling book *The 12 Week Year*.

10

CASTING AN
ACCOUNTABLE
SHADOW

There is an old adage that says: "Our actions speak louder than our words." The actions we take each day carry more weight with others than most of us realize. Politicians are famous for their speeches, and infamous for their actions (or lack thereof). Our actions, more than our statements, are a window into our true thinking. That's why being intentional with our behaviors as leaders is critical to establishing the behaviors that we want to see in our teams.

Leaders are especially positioned to influence others with their actions based on their role. People constantly look to them for insights and direction. They learn what's most important to do based on what the leader does. If the leader cuts corners, they will too; if the leader works to be excellent, they will likely do the same.

This chapter is targeted at organizational leaders, yet it is applicable for everyone. We influence our children, our peers, and even our bosses by the actions we take more than the words that we speak.

Many of our own behaviors are an outcome of observing someone else behave in a certain way in a similar situation. Research has confirmed that others' behaviors influence ours. We all can see how social influencers affect what people say, do, and wear. We all tend to emulate powerful and influential people in our lives.

Who are the first powerful people we come in contact with in life? It's mom and dad. Or if you were raised by your grandparents, then it's grandma or grandpa. Whoever was in the parenting role. Have you noticed that you imitate some characteristics from the people who raised you? You might be grateful for some of those characteristics, coping skills, or talents, others you might not be so grateful for.

Most parents have had that moment of shock (and sometimes horror!) when they hear the words they heard as a child emerge from their own mouth. Michael's daughter is a great example of this precise thing. When she was just 3 years old, she was in the hospital running a high fever. A nurse attempted to put an IV into her arm to replenish her fluid levels. The nurse was having trouble finding a vein and had to stick his daughter several times with the needle, with no success. After each failed attempt, his daughter would say to the nurse: "Stop! It hurts!"

Finally, after several tries, she said to the nurse in a loud voice: "Stop it, dumb ass!" The nurse started laughing and called someone else to hook up the IV. After the laughter stopped, Kristin (Michael's wife) was embarrassed because whenever she was cut off in traffic, or another driver did something stupid, her favorite phrase was "dumb ass." They always told their children not to swear, but their actions literally said something else.

I have found that for me, there are things my dad did that I find myself doing. I swear that it's my dad speaking through me. I feel like I'm channeling my dad at times when it comes to my children. I've always loved animals since I was very young. As a kid, I would bring home anything I could get my hands on – snakes, mice, birds, rabbits, stray dogs. My dad's response was always the same; "You're not keeping that here." Sometimes we would end up keeping it, and sometimes I would find a home for it, or release it. As a kid I remember thinking to myself, "Man, when I grow up I'm going to have all kinds of critters."

Well, interestingly enough, my kids will bring something home, and my response is very different than what I had thought it would be as a child. In fact, I hear my dad's words coming out of my mouth, "You're not keeping that here." There are many other characteristics I have from my mom and dad as well, some positive and a few that make me pause. I'm sure the same is true for you. I'm sure if you think about it, you can identify a few characteristics you have that came directly from one of your parents. And it wasn't that they taught you that per se – you just picked up on it.

My wife, Judy, and I are pretty intentional about creating a family identity for our children, because we know that matters. It will help to shape who they become, and it will help them in moments when faced with critical decisions to have that foundation – but so much of that happens unintentionally. It happens just by them watching and experiencing. Because you can say one thing, but if you're doing something else, you know that what you are doing has the greater influence. That's the walk. It's not enough to just talk the talk; you have to walk it. Others need to see it in action.

You may remember this little poem titled "Children Learn What They Live." It goes like this:

> If children live with Criticism, they learn to condemn.
> If they live with Hostility, they learn to fight.
> With Shame, they learn guilt.
> If Tolerance, they learn to be patient.
> If they live with Encouragement, they find confidence.
> Praise, they learn to appreciate.

I remember this time, I was around 9 years old, and my mom, my younger sister Pam, and I went to the mall shopping. We started in Sears (the largest retailer in the country at the time), and after some time we walked out into the mall to visit some of the other stores. We didn't get more than a few feet out when a man came out from Sears and stopped us. He flashed a badge and said to Mom, "Ma'am, I need to talk with you. Your daughter stole a piece of candy." Apparently, he was a plainclothes security officer for Sears. Back in its heyday, Sears had a fairly large candy department that included a self-serve section where you would choose what you wanted, bag it, and take it to the register and pay for it.

Well, it seems my sister had helped herself to a piece of candy without paying. Pam was around 5 years old, and when the officer confronted Mom, Pam immediately pointed directly at me and said, "He took some, too!" Not willing to go down alone, I blurted out, "Well, Dad takes it all the time!"

I can only imagine that the officer was feeling like this was a red banner day, having just busted a crime family that was the primary cause of shrinkage at his store.

The truth is, we had seen Dad take a piece practically every time we visited the store – Dad loved his sweets. What we didn't see was that he would put the money on the counter. Sometimes when people don't see you doing the right thing, they can make assumptions. Make your important actions visible to others whenever possible.

Michael and his family traveled to Europe when he was 14. Back then, tickets were paper based, and each time that you got on a flight, they would pull the part of the ticket for that leg of the journey. The paper tickets had value; they were as good as cash until the gate agent pulled them. The thing is that the gate agent in Ireland didn't pull the tickets for the return flights to New York. In essence, Michael's dad could have cashed in his tickets for the four of them and saved a ton of money.

As Michael recounts the story, "The amazing thing is, as soon as my dad noticed the error, he went up to the gate agent boarding our flight in New York and said, 'They forgot to pull my tickets.' I was with my dad when he did this, and the gate agent stopped and looked at my dad with an expression on his face like he just saw Bigfoot. He then said three words I will never forget: 'An honest man!'"

Michael remembers a lot from that trip, but what he recalls most is his dad's behavior on that return journey. Since that day, Michael has strived to live up to his dad's standard of honesty and integrity.

Yes, we emulate powerful people in our lives, and it starts with family. But that's not the only place it happens. It's not just at home; it's also at work with your leaders. If you think about powerful people in your work life, they are often the leaders. As a result, every organization is in some key ways a reflection of the leader. The leader casts a shadow for the entire organization.

His or her qualities and traits and how they behave, more than anything they say, influences and shapes the organization.

As I think about the organizations I've worked in over my career, the people I've admired, the powerful people who were my bosses, I have adopted some of the characteristics that those leaders lived. Looking back to UPS where I started in college, I worked for a gentleman who was a great motivator, and I really emulated that. I watched what he did, I tried to do similar things. I learned a ton from just watching how he operated. And to this day, I still role model some of the things he did. Things I just naturally picked up by watching him. He didn't pull me aside and say, hey, this is how you motivate people. I just watched how he did it and how people responded.

On the flipside, he could also play the victim. He complained a lot about things that were outside of his control. And I remember I picked up on that pretty quickly, too. Unfortunately, I carried that habit into the next company I joined, and I had to quickly get a handle on it. Because my new boss was not a victim at all, and it was a completely different culture.

But there's always positives in most leaders and cultures, and some not so positives. The point is that we emulate powerful people in our lives. Who are those people at work? The leaders: you. We call this phenomenon *shadow of the leader*. Michael and I first learned about the shadow concept when we worked for Senn-Delaney Management Consultants.

As leaders, we cast shadows in our organizations. And if you've worked in more than one company, you know the culture is in large part a reflection of the leader. The culture reflects the characteristics and the priorities of the leader. The organizational traits shadow those of the leader. Whether you're aware of it or not, your organization is being shaped by how you behave, by your shadow. You're influencing the organization – the priorities, how team members behave, what gets rewarded, what gets praised, what gets emphasized – by your behavior more than anything you say. That's the concept of shadow of the leader.

The shadow effect is ever present and powerful in every organization, big or small. This is why the way you view accountability has enormous repercussions within your company. If you hold the traditional view of accountability, that will have a ripple effect throughout the company, and as we pointed out in an earlier chapter, it will affect the other values as well.

The minute you say, "We need to do a better job of holding our employees accountable," you have set in motion a chain of beliefs and actions that will ultimately end in leaders employing negative consequences in an effort to get employees to perform to standard. And when you, yourself, role model the hold-them-accountable practices, you have cemented it as an acceptable and endorsed way of operating.

Your actions have shown the organization exactly how you expect the leaders at every level to manage and confront underperforming team members. Essentially, your actions are loudly saying, "We will not tolerate poor performance and will punish anyone who underperforms." This creates a wave of ongoing actions that actually undermine performance and can destroy morale. As performance continues to lag and morale decreases, the leaders have no choice but to turn up the frequency and intensity of the hold-them-accountable consequences, virtually guaranteeing mediocre results and pushback. All of this is triggered by *YOUR ACTIONS* as the leader.

The shadow concept can be a nemesis or a friend. As a leader, you cast a long shadow. Much of this is likely positive and productive, but as we've discussed, the prevailing view of accountability as consequence management is unproductive and damaging. The good news is this: The quickest and most effective way to change your culture is to change your shadow. The only way to effectively and permanently change the shadow your actions create is to first change how you view accountability.

As we pointed out, your actions are always an outgrowth of your thinking. You can try and "act" a certain way, but unless your thinking aligns and supports those actions, you will struggle to be consistent with them. It takes a massive amount of effort to act in a way that is incongruent with your thoughts and beliefs. And in times of stress, your actions will almost always revert back to being in alignment with your underlying thinking. Unless you change how you, and your leaders, view accountability, your organization will struggle to do anything other than apply a consequence-driven model.

You set the stage. Lee Iacocca, the automotive executive, once said, "The speed of the leader is the speed of the team." That's the shadow concept. The team emulates and follows the leader. You can dramatically change the company by casting a different shadow – a shadow based on the understanding of accountability as choice, as ownership. Change how you think and you will change how you act, which in turn will powerfully help change how your entire organization behaves.

11

PUTTING IT ALL TOGETHER

INTRODUCTION

We have tried in the previous chapters to contrast the differences as we see them between the traditional definition of accountability and what we refer to as Uncommon Accountability based on personal ownership. We believe that ownership of one's choices is at the heart of true accountability. Most individuals intuitively understand accountability as a personal character trait, a discipline to make good choices and to take productive action, yet people who struggle with accountability often don't trust themselves to make productive decisions consistently. They often have low self-efficacy, not believing that they will do what it takes to accomplish their goals, but rather that they *won't* do those things.

In Chapter 1, I told a quick story about how we helped my daughter, at an early age, learn to make productive choices based on their likely consequences. As parents or influencers of children or teenagers, we can have a huge impact on the course of their lives by helping them understand the cause-and-effect relationships between their choices and the lives they will lead in the future.

Research shows that a few of the choices we make early in life can set us on a path of outcomes and consequences that don't come to full fruition until decades into the future. The high school years are a particularly critical time where independence grows and adult influence wanes. A few choices made at this time of life will have a significant and long-lasting effect on life-time economics.

The Brookings Institute has studied the issue of poverty in great depth. In 2013, it identified three key choices teens and young adults can make to avoid a likely lifetime of poverty:[1]

1. Choose to stay in school and graduate.
2. Choose to wait to marry and have children until after 21.
3. Find full-time employment and stay employed.

For some, family, economic, and societal challenges make these choices harder than for others; yet if a teen does these three things, the chance of them falling into a lifetime of poverty is just 2%, and there is a 74% chance of being in the middle class or above. It's not that it is statistically impossible to recover in life; it's just that it takes a significant and sustained effort with much lower odds of success than it would to make the better choice in the first place.

High schoolers need to know these facts and understand that if they choose to drop out or have children before marriage, they are also choosing the long-term outcomes and consequences that go hand-in-glove with their behavior choice.

Whether or not they made good choices in high school, adults who struggle to make productive choices, often seek out someone to "hold them accountable." That may sound like a positive attribute, and many leaders love to hear that phrase, yet that isn't what taking ownership means. That low-efficacy

---

[1] Ron Haskins, "Three Simples Rules Poor Teens Should Follow to Join the Middle Class," Brookings (March 13, 2013), https://www.brookings.edu/opinions/three-simple-rules-poor-teens-should-follow-to-join-the-middleclass/.

approach is based on giving up choice and control. In fact, it relies on someone else to drive their success. Interestingly, since most managers apply consequence management, those same performers who want to be held accountable often also begin to resent and resist their managers over time.

The mindset (either consciously or unconsciously) of most managers who rely on consequences to hold others accountable is that their direct reports cannot be trusted to do the productive things without the imminent promise and threat of consequences. This lack of professional trust is both patronizing and caustic. If a team member can't be trusted without management oversight, you have the wrong team member. On the other hand, if they are trustworthy, they will see the consequence model for what it is – a lack of trust in their ability and integrity to do the productive thing. That relationship is antithetical to the development of high-performance team cultures.

In the final assessment, individuals who have taken ownership of their own lives and their professional success accomplish more and have more well-being than those who do not. Leaders who foster true accountability as ownership with their teams statistically outperform their peers who do not.

In this final chapter, we will discuss what ownership is and how to recognize it. Then we will outline how you can apply the concept on Uncommon Accountability, first as an individual and then as a leader.

WHAT IS OWNERSHIP, AND HOW DO YOU RECOGNIZE IT?

How can you tell when someone has taken psychological ownership of their role? What behaviors do they exhibit? How is their thinking unique? How are their actions different from a typical employee? How are their results different from others' without ownership? At its core, these questions are what this book is about.

What does ownership look like? Bring to mind someone you have met who clearly had an ownership approach to what they were engaged in. Maybe it was that doctor in the emergency room when your daughter was running a 105-degree temperature who talked to you and your child in a way that showed he cared and was on top of your situation and also on top of all the other demands on his time. Maybe it was the real estate agent who you could tell genuinely cared more about what was best for you than about optimizing their commissions. Or maybe it was that car wash attendant who showed more commitment to delivering on their mission at an exceptional level than people being paid 10 times as much.

Ownership may be hard to define, but we know it when we see it. Owners own everything about their role. Owners don't stop at the defined edge of their job description; they have ownership of the entire mission. It's the Lyft driver who has cold bottles of water for their passenger, it's the homeowner who picks up the can that was thrown in front of a neighbor's house, it's the lawn care professional who tells you that they damaged your fence (when most likely you wouldn't have noticed it or known it was them) and replaces the broken parts the next time they cut your grass. They see the bigger purpose in what they do and see it as their responsibility to deliver on that purpose.

Owners embrace high standards and expect that others will, too. Owners have taken stewardship of their various roles in life – they take the initiative to make decisions that are in line with the accomplishment of their mission. They give discretionary effort, sometimes at a personal sacrifice. Owners may break the rules when there is a higher calling to do so.

Think about it – do you want a doctor who has to be held accountable to work to the letter of insurance protocols, or one who has taken ownership of her Hippocratic oath? Do you want a bus driver for your children to be held accountable for his on-time performance, or one who has taken ownership of his efficiency *and* his responsibility to keep his passengers safe?

Ownership is not an outcome that is possible through holding people accountable, or being held accountable. You may get compliance to minimum standards, but who wants their neurosurgeon to perform to minimum standards?

Holding capable means that performers can identify breakdowns and also be creative problem solvers within the constraints of the system they are in. In World War II, British pilots, hearing that the British and American troops in Normandy were unable to get beer to drink, found a way to retrofit the surplus fuel tank holders on the wings of their spitfires to drop modified beer kegs near the troops to help keep up morale. This was certainly not a job requirement of the pilots (in fact the British government tried to stop it at one point); they did it to help win the war by cheering up the troops with the unofficial approval of the higher command. The pilots served a larger purpose than their job descriptions to further the cause of winning the war. That's ownership.[2]

People who have taken ownership find fulfillment in the work, and they take satisfaction in performing up to the high standards of excellence that they have embraced. If you want

---

[2] This is how British pilots made beer runs for troops in Normandy. James Elphick, February 8, 2019, on wearethemighty.com.

owners, stop trying to hold your people accountable and instead hold them capable.

PUTTING IT ALL TOGETHER – INDIVIDUAL
WHERE ARE YOU ON THE ACCOUNTABILITY–VICTIM SPECTRUM?

If you are personally seeking to gain greater levels of accountability in your life in order to experience greater success and fulfillment, the only place to start from is where you are right now. Take a few minutes to determine where you fall on the victim–accountability spectrum. This is not an absolute scale; it really is just an assessment for you to decide what areas you want to work on. As we have said, no one is 100% victim or accountable. We all live our lives somewhere in between; it's the direction that we are headed in that matters.

One of the hardest things to do in life is to confront the truth about ourselves. The problem is, though, that if we can't confront reality, we can never change it. Every journey, whether mental or physical, must start from where you stand. It isn't always easy to confront the truth about ourselves. We'd all like to start from a spot closer to our goals, but that choice isn't an option. Sometimes the truth hurts – we often resist it and sometimes resent it, but the only way to change it is to know it.

If you are ready to dig into where you fall on the spectrum, put bookmarks in Chapters 1 through 4. Those chapters dig into aspects of the victim and accountable mindsets, and they may help you to see how you show up in those areas.

Let's start with the benefits and costs of an accountable life stance discussed in Chapters 1 and 3. The benefits of accountability read like an aspirational life vision: sustained career success, strong relationships, good health, confidence, growth, learning, respect, an ability to overcome setbacks, and being in demand. All of those outcomes are made much more likely with an accountable view of life; they are virtually impossible destinations with a victim mindset. Do you see sustained evidence of these things in your life? Their frequent presence in your life are strong indicators that you fall on the accountable end of the spectrum. (Although if you are significantly accountable, you probably already knew that!).

There are, of course, also prices to an accountable mindset as well. Chapter 3 starts off with a list of some common costs of being accountable. These costs can include the need to change, ego hits, acknowledgment of responsibility, personal risk, push-back from others wanting us not to change, loss of relationships with others who were hurt by our choices, loss of face, subject to blame, additional work required to get better, time lost to getting back on track, and monetary costs. Take a look at those and see if you also notice a frequent presence of these costs in your life. Again, if these prices are familiar to you, then you are likely more accountable than average.

It's time to look at the other side of the proverbial account-ability coin. Peruse the lists of the benefits, costs, behaviors, and thinking of a victim mindset spelled out in the Flawed Thinking section of Chapter 2. Check off all of the positive and negative outcomes that you experience regularly. As you review those lists, ask yourself what significant outcomes you have noticed in your life that are due to victim thinking.

The benefits of a victim mindset include: shift blame from yourself, avoid punishments and penalties, protect self-image, save face, eliminate need to change, avoid confronting painful truths, seek compensation for losses I could have avoided, min-imize workload, angle for sympathy from others. This can be a tough question to answer honestly: How many of those benefits do you frequently partake of?

Finally take a look at the costs associated with a predominantly victim mindset listed in Chapter 2. These include loss of confidence, loss of respect, loss of self-respect, reduced self-efficacy, repeated mistakes (learning is avoided), lost time, poor results compared to peers, strained relationships with those who are more accountable. Which of these costs do you have a pattern of paying?

It may help to have a visual of where you fall on the victim–accountable spectrum. Here is a quick visual you can use to place yourself approximately where you fall between the two poles in the areas of your life where being accountable is most important to you:

Health

Victim Mindset	1	2	3	4	5	6	7	8	9	10	Accountable Mindset

Career/Occupation

Victim Mindset	1	2	3	4	5	6	7	8	9	10	Accountable Mindset

Finances

Victim Mindset	1	2	3	4	5	6	7	8	9	10	Accountable Mindset

Relationships

Victim Mindset	1	2	3	4	5	6	7	8	9	10	Accountable Mindset

Other: _____

Victim Mindset	1	2	3	4	5	6	7	8	9	10	Accountable Mindset

First identify the areas in your life that mean the most to you. They don't have to be areas that others think are important; what's important is that they matter to you. However, even an area that may be less important to you might be critical for other areas of your life. For example, if you are not as healthy as you could be, it can drain energy away from other important areas such as relationships and career.

Next rank yourself on a scale of 1–10, 1 being the worst and 10 being the best. Remember that we are not using an absolute scale – the rankings are relative to where you want to be. If you rated yourself low in one or more areas, don't be discouraged. This is a guilt-free exercise. Remember, true accountability is not about blame. Every one of us falls short in some way. The point is to always work to be moving in the productive direction. Trajectory and steady progress over time matter more than your starting point. A good guideline is that any area in which you scored less than a 7 is a potential candidate for greater ownership and growth.

Don't Beat Yourself Up

One of the most unproductive types of victim thinking is the tendency to beat ourselves up for our shortcomings. Accountability isn't about blame at all. In fact, accountability is about acknowledging truth, and then deciding to act productively on that truth.

Self-blame is demoralizing, and it almost always leads to lower performance and lower energy and enthusiasm. It is a way to make a poor situation even worse. Self-blame is passive and reenforces the thinking that you are not capable. If you don't believe in your own capability, then you simply will not act on it, and you will accomplish less in life than you are ultimately capable of.

If self-blame is an issue for you, reframe your thinking to focus on past and current successes that belie your internal blame dialog. Intentionally change your self-talk to recognize how you have shown productive accountable behaviors in your past.

In addition, beyond past experiences, using self-affirmations as powerful antidotes to internal negative self-talk is also effective. Your brain can watch a fictional movie and get sad, angry, happy, and experience a variety of other feelings, even though you know that it's fiction. At one level, your brain does not make the distinction between a story and reality. Use that aspect of your brain to tell yourself positive productive stories about yourself. I am accountable, I am capable of great things, I act on what matters, I am excellent at what I do, I do what it takes, and so on.

SELF-INQUIRY

Polar opposite thinking is also a powerful tool to shift your thinking and become more open to new viewpoints that are different than your own. When looking to grow in accountability, stop feeding the thoughts that paint you as an innocent victim and be open to the ways in which you are the primary architect of your current situation.

As an example, say that you feel that your current boss is unfair to you and that you don't have the same opportunities that other people do. This mindset causes you to check out more and more and not deliver your best. You repeatedly get mediocre reviews, and you feel like the boss's "favorites" get huge passes for their mistakes and get special treatment that you don't get. Of course, if you just ask your boss how she feels about you, she might tell you her real thinking, or she might not – you don't control her openness to your question.

Whether you are right or wrong, your initial thinking is almost irrelevant – your current thinking has become a self-fulfilling prophecy. In either case, you perform below your capabilities because you have "checked-out," which contributes to your mediocre reviews. This in turn reinforces your mindset. This is why your view of accountability matters.

It's important to keep in mind that your thinking drives your actions, and your actions drive your results. The first objective is to dig into the current thinking that is driving your actions. To use polar opposite thinking to do this, write down your current belief that is creating your current results. For example, you might write: "My boss doesn't like me, and that's why she treats me unfairly." Pay attention to your feelings as you explore your mindset because they are a great signpost for your underlying unconscious beliefs.

The next step is to identify the polar opposite belief. There are usually numerous options for polar opposite thoughts. For example, it could be, "My boss thinks I am capable of more and is frustrated with me because I don't deliver like she knows I can." Another polar opposite thought might be, "My boss doesn't control how I perform, I do, and I control my own performance regardless of her thinking."

Either one of those, or some other polar opposite can work, as long as the polar opposite thinking fosters new behaviors.

The truth is you really don't know what your boss thinks, or why she behaves the way she does; so as long as you are blaming her for your performance, you are helpless to change your circumstances.

Once you have identified the appropriate polar opposite thought, the next step is to consider how it *might* be true. In fact, it may be that your boss does have conflicting beliefs about you. As your performance changes, so may her thinking. Just by considering the possibility of a new belief, your thinking opens up and it unfreezes your actions. This isn't an exercise in being right; it is an exercise in possibilities, since we can never really know what anyone else is really thinking anyway. Polar opposites might be true, they might be partially true, or they might not be true at all – you may never know for sure. The point is that you select a possibility that can open up a whole new set of potential actions that are enabled by the new thinking and that will be more productive.

As you continue to shift your thinking, identify the behaviors that align with the new thinking and act on them. Monitor the results of the new actions and adjust as needed. Soon enough, your new actions will generate results consistent with the underlying thinking.

ENQUIRY OF OTHERS

Another way to uncover how your thinking may be on the victim side of the spectrum is to ask people whom you trust what they see. Let's use the example again that you think your boss is unfair to you.

Identify one or two people who are familiar with the situation, who also have your best interest at heart. Don't pick people who are not interested in you, or who are centered on themselves in your relationships with them. Pick people who will have the courage to tell you the truth, not what you want to hear.

Ask them to give you their insights about how they see the situation, your role in creating it, and your options to change it. It may not be easy to hear everything they have to say. If it gets hard to hear, don't argue or defend – ask them open-ended questions to really dig into their insights. By staying open, letting them know that you want to hear them, and by asking questions, you will likely hear some of the most valuable insights about your thinking and actions that you have ever heard. Thank them for their insights. If they feel as if you heard them, they will be a sounding board going forward.

Don't seek to be right when you are receiving the feedback; seek to be open and honest about the truth you hear. That is one of the prices of growing in accountability. Identify the productive behaviors that are enabled by the healthier insights that you received and open up to the possibilities of what would be different if they were true. Identify the new productive actions that are associated with those beliefs and execute them. The new actions will further reinforce the new beliefs, especially as your results change for the better.

Wherever you fall on the victim–accountable spectrum, the productive approach is to always work to become more personally accountable. What we continue to develop continues to grow. What we are complacent about and ignore tends to diminish. What are your most important accountability growth opportunities?

Lastly, identify the key thinking shifts and actions needed to make progress toward greater accountability in the one or two area(s) that you picked as most important to you. Don't try to fix everything at once – that is a recipe for overwhelm and failure. The good news is that success in one area tends to create progress in the others. That's because when we start to think and act more accountably in one area it tends to positively affect all of the other areas as well. Focusing on one thing is a far more powerful force than diffusing your effort across many things.

RECOGNIZING ACCOUNTABILITY IN YOURSELF AND OTHERS

Acknowledging the areas of healthy personal accountability that exist for you today is another helpful way to build confidence and then to leverage that success in the areas where you may not be showing up as accountably. Further, recognizing your progress toward greater levels of accountability is a key part of reenforcing and accelerating your personal growth.

Recognizing accountability in others that you work with, or know in your personal life, is another key strategy in developing your intentional growth in accountability. Identifying others who are accountable starts by assessing their results. What separates their results from the rest? How do those results enable options for them that they might not otherwise have if their results were mediocre? What would be different for you, and those around you, if you could achieve their level of performance? As you begin to imagine the possibilities, your thinking automatically shifts in a productive direction.

Next, dig into how those top performers' actions differ from the behaviors of others. Be a student of how they operate.

What actions drive their results? How do they approach their work and how do they decide when they are done working each day? How do they use their time? What motivates them? How do they interact with others? How do they react to low performers? How big of a game are they playing – are they only concerned with their performance, or do they seem to care about the performance of the team, the whole company?

From what you've learned, identify how your thinking and behaviors can shift to align with those of the top performers that you have watched. Be careful, though; as we have identified, ownership comes at a price. There is more work and more commitment. And yet, ask yourself: Do those top performers look overworked? Do they look dissatisfied? On the contrary, top performers typically have higher levels of satisfaction and enthusiasm than the rest.

FINDING AND MEETING WITH ACCOUNTABILITY PEERS

In our book *The 12 Week Year*, we outline a powerful accountability reinforcer: weekly accountability meetings (WAMs). These meetings are small groups of peers who meet regularly to review individual progress and to celebrate and confront the performance results of the members. By entering into a mutually reinforcing peer group, the performance of each of the members improves, and that performance is sustained far longer than in the circumstances where people try to go it alone.

WAMs are groups of people who care about their personal performance and the performance of the other group members. Members attend the meetings consistently, they come prepared to report out on their execution and results from the previous week, they openly discuss where they were successful and where they fell short. In short, WAMs are small groups of like-minded peers who have all taken ownership for their own success. Since people tend to perform better when others are watching; accountable performers seek out productive relationships with others who are on the same trajectory as they are.

When no group is available to meet, one-to-one accountability is possible with a peer who can help us confront the situation when we fall short and recognize us when we do well – as long as we are willing to do the same for them in return. A productive accountability partnership, whether in a WAM or one on one, is a powerful tool to grow in accountability quickly.

Own Your Own Growth

Taking ownership of your growth and development is a common trait of Uncommon Accountability. Start by identifying the limiting factors in your life that are holding you back, and then identify the degrees of freedom that you have to overcome them. If you lack the skills, then determine the training and experiences you need to get better. If your comfort zone is holding you back, find ways to push through the discomfort into the growth zone with small risks and challenges that stretch you, without hitting your panic zone. Is the fear of failure holding you back? Change your thinking about what failure is – it isn't final unless you quit, because failure is a necessary element of growth. No failure, no growth. Whatever you identify as your limiting factors, confront them and take action to overcome them as part of your daily and weekly routines.

PUTTING IT ALL TOGETHER – LEADER
FEAR OF GIVING UP CONTROL

By this point, we have either made the case for holding your team capable or we haven't. What's left to do is to summarize how a leader can transition from consequences to ownership. One of the first barriers to embracing the choice/capable model of accountability is the fear that as a manager you will lose control over results.

This fear is reflective of the deeply rooted underlying belief that when people don't behave as expected you can force them to do so. Unless and until this thinking changes you will struggle to move away from consequence management and embrace the capable approach.

Consequences do in fact work to improve results; there are decades of peer-reviewed research as well as innumerable frontline examples that prove consequence management can be effective at shaping behavior (if only up to a point). The business case for confronting performers with their ability to choose seems less well supported. After all, *if consequences ain't broke, don't fix it,* right?

Except that for all of the reasons that we have covered in earlier chapters, consequence management is "broke." It cannot deliver a team of highly motivated owners who perform to high standards and don't require massive amounts of management, training, and systems support to keep it all going.

The "hold them capable" juice is definitely worth the squeeze, and as culture is rapidly changing all over the world, it is a model of leadership that is future-proof, not one that is based on the mechanical management practices of the industrial revolution of yesteryear.

Holding people capable is about confronting people with their ability make choices for themselves, to take ownership of their own success, to tap into what motivates them and what they are truly capable of in life. Consequences still play a significant role in the choice model – they're just seen as the outcomes of the choices that performers make over time, rather than consequences applied by management fiat. Managers may explain the consequences for performance and specify the actions that create those consequences, but the performer retains the choice whether to do them. That choice is to either meet the standards or choose to leave.

Holding people capable is not soft. To do it well, there must be high-performance standards, as well as ownership of one's role and the mission of the organization. In addition, there must be flexibility to make mistakes and to learn in an effort to innovate and to serve the mission. The performance levels of traditional consequence management systems are not tolerated in a company that fosters ownership at every level. Managers may feel like they have less control, and that's because in a choice model, more control is devolved to the performer – where it best belongs.

BUILDING A HIGH-PERFORMANCE OWNERSHIP CULTURE

There are critical building blocks necessary to create and maintain a high-performance culture of ownership. They define the parameters necessary for success. Ideally, these building blocks create clarity, transparency, and evidence that the organization is delivering on the organization's mission. Without these elements, holding others capable is impossible.

The essential elements and practices of the hold-capable cultural model include the following.

HIGH-PERFORMANCE STANDARDS Standards should define the performance needed to accomplish the organization's highest values and operating outcomes. High standards define success, and they describe the nonnegotiable behaviors necessary to be part of the team. They should be a stretch and yet attainable. Performers should be made aware of both the standards and the systemic consequences that will arise by achieving them or by falling short, assuming that a performer is sufficiently skilled and understands what is expected of them.

We have said this before – high standards are at the core of the capable model. They define excellence and shape critical behavior. Standards clarify what is expected from performers in return for the compensation provided. Managers are often tempted to accept performance less than standard, but the lowest level of tolerated performance becomes the de facto standard.

Another fatal blow for meaningful standards is that they are not applied fairly and equitably to everyone. Playing favorites and cutting some individuals "slack" for substandard performance will irreparably damage the culture of ownership you are trying to build. The culture of choice is a meritocracy.

Remember the effect of the shadow you cast – consistently role model the behaviors that you expect from your team. If you want high performance, be a high performer. If you want performance standards to be met consistently, meet your standards consistently. If you want people to be owners of the business, take ownership yourself.

PERFORMANCE FEEDBACK   Regular performance feedback on execution and results is essential if performers are to
optimize their outcomes. For high standards to be attained, an
information-rich environment must be present. Allowing performers to get clarity on what's working, what's not, and where
they stand relative to their goals enables the daily and weekly
adjustments to stay on track with their goals. Measurement is
an absolute requirement to hold people capable.

When providing feedback, in general positive feedback can
be delivered either publicly or privately. Generally constructive
feedback is best delivered in a one-on-one session.

Measurement systems exist in hold-accountable systems,
but they support consequence management. Measurement
in a hold-capable system is used to provide performers with
feedback about what is working and what is not, and to
provide direction on where to adjust.

CONSEQUENCES IN A HOLD-CAPABLE MODEL   Consequences exist in every system, whether designed in or as natural consequences of the value-creation process. Generally, some
consequences inhibit behaviors, others are neutral, and still others encourage behaviors. To optimize results, it is critical that
leadership ensures that both the natural and designed-in consequences are tightly aligned with the accomplishment of the
primary goals of an organization.

Leadership's role is to clearly communicate the consequences
of the performance model that result from the various choices
made by the performer. To foster ownership rather than mere
compliance, never apply consequences in anger, to punish, or to

establish control or authority. Consequences, whether positive or negative, should be seen to arise based on the choices made by the performer (assuming that they are trained and capable to perform their roles).

Consequences belong to the performer; don't apply them as a lever to improve performance. Instead, coach your team members to embrace their metrics themselves to take ownership of their choices and consequences.

OWNERSHIP CULTURE Teams and individuals that have taken ownership of their roles outperform those that have a traditional employee mindset. Employees work to the core job description; owners work to deliver their best results and live the mission.

Performers who have taken ownership identify ways to improve their processes and the business in general. They are free to make the decisions needed to perform well without getting permission first. Performers in hold-capable systems are not punished for mistakes in their effort to grow and develop. Uncommon Accountability comes with the autonomy to make the choices necessary to accomplish the goals.

TRUST YOUR TEAM
- Trust your performers to make good choices and to take ownership. (If you can't trust them, you likely have the wrong team member.)
- Establish coach–owner relationships (not boss–subordinate).
- Avoid the temptation to provide the "right answers" to your performers; instead, seek their insights and ideas.

- Meet your team members individually and outline the foundations of the ownership/choice model:
  - Their success is an outcome of the choices they make either to take the productive actions or not to take those actions.
  - Your role is not to try to force them to perform through consequences; your role is to help them acknowledge their power to choose.
  - Make explicit the consequences in the system and how their choices determine which consequences they experience. In the end, they choose their own consequences.
  - Your goal as a leader is to be a partner-coach to help them accomplish their most important goals.

COACHING TO OWNERSHIP   As a leader, coaching is the most effective way to help people to take ownership of their choices and results, and the disciplines of *The 12 Week Year* are perfectly suited to be a coaching platform to hold performers capable.

There are five core execution disciplines that provide an effective framework for coaching. Each of the five disciplines are part of *The 12 Week Year* and can create value when applied in isolation, but when applied together as a system, they drive dramatic growth.

The first of these execution disciplines is *vision*. As a leader seeking to foster ownership in my team, I absolutely need my individual team members to have a meaningful vison. A vision that enables people to reach farther into what they are capable of has at least three key benefits.

A solid vision provides consistent direction for plan development – it will help the performer to say no to some things and yes to others, depending upon the alignment with their vision. A good vision also stretches the boundaries of what is possible for the performer. By setting a stretch vision, a performer will accomplish more than if they had a vision that was too small or too easy. A well-written vision also creates an emotional response in the performer. The vision should create the excitement and desire needed to take the uncomfortable actions in the plan that are necessary to hit the short-term goals – which in turn represent progress toward the long-term vision.

The second execution discipline is *planning*. A solid plan has two key elements: a goal that represents needed progress toward the vision and is also a great outcome in itself, and the critical few tactics necessary to hit the goal. We find that the best planning cycle for execution is 12 weeks long – enough time to make progress, but not so much time that change and uncertainty in the competitive space make the plan obsolete.

The third and fourth disciplines taken together are *process control* and *scorekeeping*. Process control is a set of tools and events that help you to execute the tactics in your plan at a pace sufficient for you to reach your goal. The two key tools of process control are a written weekly plan that contains only the tactics due in the current week and a WAM with peers. The scorekeeping discipline tracks both the weekly execution score and a set of leading and lagging progress metrics. By keeping score, the performer knows exactly where they stand each week and what, if any, adjustments are needed.

The final discipline is *time use*. Each week, the performer works from a time-blocked weekly calendar that carves out time to execute the tactics in their plan as well as for administrative and emergent activities.

LEADER AS COACH PROCESS

1. Start with what they want from their role and what their vision for the future looks like.
2. Clarify that your role is to help them as a coach; the burden to perform is theirs.
3. Explain the standards and the consequences for performance and nonperformance.
4. Let them know that you will be meeting with them regularly to discuss their progress, confront breakdowns, discuss their ideas, and identify action steps.
5. Schedule a recurring coaching time to meet with them and discuss progress and adjustments.
6. In each coaching session, review their progress and jointly identify needed adjustments that might be warranted.

BENEFITS OF AN OWNERSHIP CULTURE

*   Organization has higher employee satisfaction and retains the best talent.
*   Relationships are strong, productive, and open.
*   Leaders are freed of the time-consuming and unpleasant burden of delivering consequences, which enables a wider leadership span.

CONCLUSION

How you view accountability affects everything that you do and accomplish. Seeing accountability as something that can be forced creates a mindset of "have to." For example: *I have to call 100 leads per day every day or I will be let go*, versus *I choose to work here, so by default I am choosing the performance standards as well.*

The work is the same, but the two mindsets are polar opposites. The first mindset feels like you are trapped, you are powerless, a victim to circumstances. You have no choice but to do what you dislike. The second mindset is one of choice, and that mindset is one of ownership and of Uncommon Accountability.

The work is the same, it's just the amount of control and freedom you have in the second way of thinking is infinitely greater. You always have choice. You might not like the choices that are available, but you always, always have choice. And that keeps control in your hands where it belongs.

Uncommon Accountability is a life stance, a mindset that is no long-term victim to circumstance. It is set on the bedrock of the ability to choose in any circumstance. Jean-Paul Sartre said, "There are two ways to go to the gas chamber, free or not free." If there is choice on the way to the gas chamber, then there is choice in our work, our relationships, and in our lives, and that is all we need to live a life of intention and capability.

ABOUT THE AUTHORS

BRIAN P. MORAN

Brian is a leading authority on leadership, execution, and productivity. As CEO and founder of The Execution Company, Brian is a highly respected expert and accomplished executive and entrepreneur.

Brian is the co-author of the *New York Times* bestseller *The 12 Week Year*, a program developed to empower individuals and companies to achieve more in 12 weeks than what others accomplish in 12 months. Brian consults with many of the top executives and largest companies in the world.

Prior to launching The Execution Company, Brian held leadership positions with PepsiCo, UPS, Senn-Delaney Management Consultants, and National Automotive Corporation. Coupling his corporate experience with his entrepreneurial drive, Brian also launched a number of start-up ventures, including co-founded Bio-Inc., a health services provider specializing in wellness and medical surveillance performing onsite medical testing.

In addition to *The 12 Week Year*, Brian has authored three other best-selling books, is featured in many of the leading business journals and periodicals, and speaks extensively around the globe.

Brian resides in Arizona and Michigan with his wife, Judy, and their two daughters, Gabrielle and Emma.

MICHAEL LENNINGTON

Michael is a leading expert in the application of execution systems for individuals, teams, and entire organizations. Currently, he spends his professional time training and coaching his entrepreneurial clients, writing about leadership and business execution, and building simple tools for people seeking to accomplish more in business and in life.

What has driven Michael's work since the beginning is helping others overcome the thinking and action barriers that keep them from accomplishing what they are capable of. He is a *New York Times* best-selling co-author of three books: *The 12 Week Year*, *The 12 Week Year Field Guide*, and *The 12 Week Year for Writers*.

Michael lives in the Greater Louisville, Kentucky, area with his wife Kristin, their three dogs, and a retired barn cat named Bean. Michael can be contacted directly at Michael@12WeekYear.com or by visiting michaellennington .com.

For additional resources visit www.uncommonaccountability .com.

To inquire about having Brian or Michael speak at your next conference email us at info@uncommonaccountability.com.

ADDITIONAL BOOKS FROM
THE AUTHORS

Available at Amazon, Barnes & Noble, your favorite bookstore, or 12weekyear.com:

In this groundbreaking book, Brian Moran and Michael Lennington unlock the simple secrets to help you accomplish more.

The 12 Week Year is a process forged in the field of sports, used by world-class athletes, and transformed for business and everyday life.

Accomplish more in 12 weeks than most do in 12 months with *The 12 Week Year*!

Are you ready to change your life? This hands-on template for implementing advice from the game-changing book *The 12 Week Year* is a study guide that makes it easy for anyone to apply the 12 week year to their own lives.

Instead of getting bogged down in annualized thinking that produces pitfalls and saps productivity, follow along with this guide to redefine your "year" to be just 12 weeks long. By doing so, you'll avoid complacency, begin to focus on what matters most, create better clarity, and develop a sense of urgency so that "now" is always the right time to act.

To help you achieve your writing goals, we partnered with Trevor Thrall, a professor at George Mason University, to write *The 12 Week Year for Writers*. Trevor, an early adopter of our process, has been using the 12 Week Year for almost 20 years to get his research and writing done and to help his students to do the same.

The book offers a comprehensive approach to help you get more high-quality words on the page than you ever thought possible.

INDEX